GREAT WRITERS BARBARA KINGSOLVER

GREAT WRITERS

BARBARA KINGSOLVER

Linda Wagner-Martin

Foreword by David King Dunaway

CHELSEA HOUSE
PUBLISHERS
A Haights Cross Communications Company

Philadelphia

CHELSEA HOUSE PUBLISHERS

VP, NEW PRODUCT DEVELOPMENT Sally Cheney
DIRECTOR OF PRODUCTION Kim Shinners
CREATIVE MANAGER Takeshi Takahashi
MANUFACTURING MANAGER Diann Grasse

Staff for BARBARA KINGSOLVER

EXECUTIVE EDITOR: Matt Uhler
ASSOCIATE EDITOR: Susan Naab
EDITORIAL ASSISTANT: Sharon Slaughter
PRODUCTION EDITOR: Megan Emery
SERIES AND COVER DESIGNER: Takeshi Takahashi
COVER: Steven Hopp © 2003
LAYOUT: EJB Publishing Services

http://www.chelseahouse.com

First Printing

9 8 7 6 5 4 3 2 1

Library of Congress Cataloging-in-Publication Data

Wagner-Martin, Linda.
  Barbara Kingsolver / Linda Wagner-Martin.
     p. cm. — (Great writers)
  Includes bibliographical references.
  ISBN 0-7910-7846-9
  1. Kingsolver, Barbara. 2. Novelists, American—20th century—Biography.
3. Women and literature—United States—History—20th century. I. Title.
II. Great writers (Philadelphia, Pa.)
  PS3561.I496Z95 2004
  813'.54—dc22
                                    2004005694

For Paul and Carly

◼ TABLE OF CONTENTS

AFTERWORD

I come from that generation that really got a chance to vote with our feet, to make something happen; and I feel like we've never quite gotten over it. If I see something wrong I have to fix it. Whether it's a leak in my bathroom or a law-breaking government I feel like I have to fix it I don't have a choice.
                                        —Barbara Kingsolver, 1992

BARBARA KINGSOLVER'S WORK has reached into 23 languages and 65 countries, a great leap for a skinny, bookish girl who "didn't think of books as having been written by people like me."*

Kingsolver's list of achievements is a long one and stretches beyond literary production. Whether endowing a literary fellowship for politically-engaged writing, crafting a half-dozen best-sellers, or playing keyboard in a writers' rock band, The Rock Bottom Remainders, Barbara Kingsolver has a voice all her own. Kingsolver has a genius for offering home truths in an accessible fashion. To popular fiction, she brings clarity and conscience. To the essay, she brings a vitality and authenticity which it has lost in recent years. It could be said of her what Jacques Barzun said of Aldous Huxley, that he was a good novelist but a great essayist.

Kingsolver is today a popular and highly regarded author of a fiction driven by passion and a scientific curiosity, seeking a "scent of the real," as Linda Wagner-Martin reflects in this eloquent volume.

An example: in Kingsolver's second novel, *Animal Dreams*, her main character Cody attends a deer dance at an unnamed pueblo in the American Southwest, at the invitation of her boyfriend. Kingsolver's description of the ritual is vivid and precise. "When I am representing cultures other than my own, I have to be really careful to get my facts straight....to write that pueblo scene, I did several things—one is read everything there was to do in the library about that ethnography and cultural background of the pueblo people(s) and then of course I went to that pueblo and I saw those dances and I also talked to people to whom those dances were very important...."

You can write about something from the outside or the inside. I write about Native American characters from the outside, but I've never written one from the inside. I know what those deer dances look like because I saw them. I feel I have a right to describe that. I have no idea what that one woman was thinking as she stood in that black dress, in the snow, barefoot. I have no idea how those men felt when they became deer."

Like novelist Cormac McCarthy, Barbara Kingsolver is a S x SW type, a meeting of Southern and Southwest identities. One might credit her Southern side with her preoccupation with society, and her Southwestern side with attention to the land and its diverse peoples.

Kingsolver's literary trajectory moves from journals kept as a child to training in scientific writing, to sharp truths about popular writing: "It's emotion not event that creates a dynamic response in a reader." (51) Her journey has taken her from anonymity to highly sought after novelist (and keyboardist to Stephen King and Amy Tan); then from fame to hard-protected privacy: "Really, sometimes my readers go too far. They think that what I write is how I live; and that I have this hot Apache boyfriend," she told me one blustery November in Tucson, a city winter rarely visits.

Kingsolver gives interviews, but not nearly so many as other best-selling novelists, for whom publicity can be as rewarding as literary art. Kingsolver prefers to present her autobiography in essay form, as reflective moral tales in essay collections such as *High Tide in Tucson* and *Small Wonder*.

This has left small mysteries to her biography, such as why she chose to move to Arizona; or why her personal legend relies on an extremely rustic view of her childhood as a doctor's daughter in Carlisle, Kentucky—a town no more than 50 miles from the state's capital and seat of its university, Lexington. (Her childhood included listening to classical music stations on the radio.)

"I moved to Arizona on a whim, in 1977," she told me. "I had been living in Europe seeking my fortune, then it got really hard to renew my work visa, so I had to move back to the states, and I'd never been to the Southwest; so I thought I'd give it a try. It's not a very grown-up-sounding answer, but maybe I wasn't a very grown-up person at the time," she laughs.

If there are mysteries to her motivations and private life, there is certainly no doubt about the way her work has been politically engaged. "Critics do say that and I never stop being surprised by it…when I write a novel, I am not thinking that, 'how can I get political themes in this'."

"It just grows out of the world that I live in, which happens to be full of sexism and racism and screwed-up immigration policies, and people who use power against other people in unjust ways—that's just the world I live in. If I lived in another world, I would write an entirely different kind of novel, I suppose."

I asked her what it meant when people called her writing "political."

"That's a confusing word—what does it mean? I think I finally figured it out during the Gulf War. Some friends of mine wanted to set up a table in a shopping mall and distribute information on the less-cheerful aspects of the Gulf War. The administrator of the mall said, 'No, you can't do that.' And my friends said, 'Well, why not'—because these people over here are setting up tables everyday and passing out yellow ribbons and bumper stickers that say, 'We kick butt'."

"And the administrators of the mall said, 'Well, yes, they can do that because what they are doing is public service; and what you are doing is 'political'. So, bingo! I understood exactly why my work is called political. It's not a public service. It's reminding people what's the matter, and that maybe they ought to think about that."

Some writers have always seen their job as giving voice to unpopular but worthy causes. "The political duty of the writer is to describe the world we live in as not being inevitable," said the English critic John Berger. "We live in a world in which we're surrounded by a very tall and gigantic wall, almost invisible, which cuts us off from any really different future."[2] Authors such as Kingsolver remind us of what's beyond, what we could hope for; and that's a legitimate—even central—function of art. As one of Kingsolver's childhood friends, musician Pete Seeger, sings, "If music alone could change the world, I'd only be a musician."

Barbara Kingsolver's reputation rose with her first three novels, intense tales of women fleeing an older, controlling lifestyle by heading out West. Ironically, this westering instinct parallels one of the oldest formats of western fiction, the Zane Gray plot of the lady from the East, Miss Kitty, who disembarks at the Santa Fe train station in awe and trepidation of her surroundings. When Kingsolver's characters today pull off the freeway, or get off the bus, they give a feminist turn to an old tale.

"I sure never thought of Zane Gray as being my literary progenitor. You are right that coming West implies (particularly for women) a chance to maybe burn the corset and start over…. All my stories are cowboys and Indians in a certain way, people who have been on the land, and people who are trying to make a mark on it from outside; and people finding their place somewhere in between these extremes."

Authors of literary forewords are fond of speculating on author's themes but rarely does the author have the chance to talk back to such characterizations. This is one of the great advantages of what I've called "Oral Literary History,' 'situating authors' work in context via their own words.[3]

"Everything that I write really comes down to an exploration of community," Kingsolver told me. "What is community? How do we fit into it? How do we hold our place and lose ourselves to something bigger in time? I think that is the only question I am ever going to try and answer…. When I studied literature in high school, I learned that there are three great themes in literature: man against man, man against nature, man against himself. So it was all 'man against' and so much of my life has no 'against' in it, whatsoever. It's mostly 'with.' I know that is not one of the great themes of literature, 'cuz it wasn't on the blackboard in Ms. Harney's class."

"Doris Lessing wrote about such women, whose goals in life were not to escape from connectedness with humanity, but to become connected; and to find a way not to lose themselves at the same time. I think that's what a lot of us women write about— 'connectedness' instead of 'againstness'."

The roots of 'connectedness' reach deep into the life of Kingsolver and her characters, who struggle with finding home. It is the struggle of the outsider, whether in the Sonoran desert or the Appalachian piedmont, to connect with the surrounding land and its community. Connectedness is also an outgrowth of Kingsolver's life-long study of ecology, in which she was trained in college and graduate school, which this volume makes clear.

In this book, Linda Wagner-Martin has given the reader the ultimate gift of biographer to reader: a balance between work and life. For those seeking the woman behind the writer, and a writer behind the woman, this volume will be a joy. Wagner-Martin's work in finding a unity of life and work is doubly appropriate to her subject. Just as Barbara Kingsolver brings connectedness to her readers, so Wagner-Martin captures a passionate and unapologetic personality, whose books have enriched the lives of millions.

Kingsolver's biographer emphasizes the influence and pull of the British novelist Doris Lessing. There are many ways in which Lessing's work resonates with Kingsolver: her writings about Africa (which Kingsolver visited as a child discussed in *The Poisonwood Bible*); and her feminism and political radicalism. Besides these *isms*, both authors share an intimate knowledge of the importance of the written word's transformative powers. Perhaps I could say of Barbara Kingsolver what Doris Lessing says of her protagonist Martha Quest, near the end of her five-volume *Children of Violence* Series:

She knew very well this area of the human mind where the machinery of ordinary life seemed more than absurd, seemed a frightening trap.... She knew that if a person were to take one word, and listen; or a pebble or a jewel and look at it; the word would give up in the end, its own meaning and the meaning of everything.[4]

David King Dunaway
April 2004

Barbara Kingsolver grew into her life as writer from wide-ranging bases of experience and knowledge. A woman who loved the lush forests of her Kentucky childhood, the austere and crisp-edged desert of her years as a young professional in Arizona, and the remote environs of wildlife preserves, Kingsolver has lived a life more private than public. For all her established fame as a novelist, she prefers the quiet of a somewhat reclusive existence.

There are, however, no ivory towers in Kingsolver's landscape. Her reclusiveness is the chosen comfort of a writer who works hard at her craft but who also insists that only her two daughters, her husband, her parents and siblings, and her friends make up her intimate world. Never to be alone in any sinister or selfish way, the writer must partake of the fullness of life. Human relationships are the webs of nourishment the writer, particularly, needs. As Kingsolver wrote recently, "I believe in parables. I navigate life using stories where I find them, and I hold tight to the ones that tell me new kinds of truth.... I create imagined lives. I write about people, mostly, and the things they contrive to do for, against, or with one another. I write about the likes of liberty, equality, and world peace, on an extremely domestic scale." (Kingsolver, *Small Wonder,* 6, 37)

One of the reasons Kingsolver's novels have such wide readership is just this recognition. Characters, though imaginative and imaginary, must have the luster, the scent, of the real. Readers read for the real, and for characters conversant with the joy and the pain of all living, but they also read to connect the best of fictional characters with their creator, the writer herself. Literature exists because readers yearn to identify—with characters and, through them, with authors.

Barbara Kingsolver's steady presence on bestseller lists since her surprisingly successful first novel, *The Bean Trees* in 1988 (now available in more than 65 countries and 23 languages), shows that her aim was itself a steady, and steadying, purpose: although never an English major, after college Kingsolver had created her own apprenticeship. She knew she would write: she had already published dozens of articles, as well as poems and stories, when she began writing *The Bean Trees*.

After she had interrupted her study toward the doctorate in ecological biology in order to take a position as a science and grant writer at her university, she became, as well, a practicing journalist—investing years of her life into covering the 1983–84 Phelps Dodge copper mine strike. The strike was an effort that lasted for nearly two years in the Arizona desert—and changed the practices of United States labor negotiation forever. To cover that story successfully, Kingsolver taped hundreds of hours of interviews with the strikers, male and female, and their spouses—and the book she eventually wrote about the conflict stemmed from these extensive oral histories. In this years-long effort, Kingsolver showed the kind of direction she would find worth taking: she had no publisher for the work and had seen in print only her brief article about the strike (in *The Progressive* magazine) along with the occasional story she had published in local newspapers. She was devoting her talent and energy to the project not in order to become a best-selling writer, but to give voice to what she believed was the injustice done to the residents of Clifton, Morenci, Douglas, and Ajo, Arizona. Kingsolver's belief system is part idealistic, part political, and many parts self-negating: she believes in both finding and expressing truths that go beyond the narrowly personal; she continuously reflects on the larger world scene.

Her nonfiction book about the strike, *Holding the Line: Women in the Great Arizona Mine Strike of 1983*, was published by a university press the year following *The Bean Trees*. In fact, she used the modest HarperCollins advance for the novel, which she had written during bouts of insomnia throughout her first pregnancy, to take the next year off—time which she spent with her newborn daughter, as well as immersed in the strikers' stories. In that year, she developed the habits of concentration for her writing which she recently described: "Several summers ago on the cabin porch, surrounded by summertime yard sales and tobacco auctions, I wrote about *Africa*, for heaven's sake. I wrote long and hard and well until I ended each day panting and exhilarated, like a marathon runner.... I didn't need to be in Africa as I wrote that book; I needed to be someplace where I could think straight, remember, and properly invent...." (*Small Wonder*, 37)

At times "in a rocking chair on the porch, or at a small blue desk facing the window," Kingsolver writes "a good deal by hand, on paper." (*Small Wonder*, 34) She uses a computer for much of her work, but the intimacy of contact, of being part of the process, is important for her. The writer is one who *conveys* as well as one who creates, and there is a sense of the spiritual in a great deal of Kingsolver's commentary about writing. Often asked about her philosophies and her processes, she takes such questions seriously. "It's a curious risk, fiction," she once said. "... In the final accounting, a hundred different truths are likely to reside at any given address. The part of my soul that is driven to make stories is a fierce thing, like a ferret: long, slack, incapable of sleep, it digs and bites through all I know of the world." (Kingsolver, *High Tide in Tucson*, 43)

But to temper this somewhat sinister sense of the writer whose aim is to reach the truth, even if that truth is unpleasant, she adds, "[F]iction works, if it does, only when we the readers believe every word of it. Grover's Corners is Our Town, and so is Cannery Row, and Lilliput, and Gotham City, and Winesburg, Ohio, and the dreadful metropolis of 1984." (*High Tide in Tucson*, 44)

It is an advantage for readers of Barbara Kingsolver's work that this author is also a reader. She can put herself in the reader's chair, because she has grown up reading—reading even more than writing. Kingsolver herself is clear in her beliefs and her expression of them, identifiable as a writer we can believe, her work easy to both imagine and assimilate. A comparatively shy woman, the tall and inherently modest Kingsolver approaches her readers as if with hands outstretched. Palms turned upward, she makes the reader's journey to understanding an easy movement from the cold print of words to the warm touch of empathy. Taylor, Lou Ann, or Turtle, Codi or Homer, Lusa or Garnett—Kingsolver's characters are the separate traits of plausible figures bundled, sometimes with the untidiness of the natural, into a pastiche of recognition.

CHAPTER ONE

A Kentucky Childhood

When I was a child, I had two parents who loved
me without cease. One of them attended every
excuse for attention I ever contrived, and the other
made it to the ones with higher production values,
like piano recitals and appendicitis.

—Barbara Kingsolver, *High Tide in Tucson*

AS BARBARA KINGSOLVER THINKS about her childhood, which she
often does now that she is rearing her own two children, she
emphasizes characteristics that—in her memory and in her practices today—seem paramount. The first is the security of having
parents who loved her unconditionally. By Kingsolver's account,
her parents, Virginia Lee Henry Kingsolver and Wendell Kingsolver, were not particularly lenient with her or her two siblings;
they ran a modest intellectual and musical household. They
intended all three of their children to be well-educated, and to
lead lives that suited them, as well as "contributing" to life. Dr.
Kingsolver, with his medical degree from the University of
Michigan, had chosen a practice that was somewhat like a min-
istry; he served the people of Nicholas County, an area of poor
farms, not unlike when he had chosen to live both in Africa and
on a Caribbean island to provide modern medical care for people

who might otherwise not have access to it. His life, both medical and personal, illustrates what his daughter has called "his drive to matter in the world." (Kingsolver–Wagner-Martin interview, 2003)

The Kingsolvers believed that children should learn to work and study, to appreciate the natural world as well as the world of museums and libraries, and to find out things for themselves through reading—the house was filled with books. They also believed in letting each child mature at his or her own pace. Kingsolver, in describing her "blessed" childhood, focuses more often on the role of her mother, because she was at home with the children: "My mother had kids to contend with from dawn till doom. She was (is) educated, creative, and much of the time the only people around for her to talk with had snakes in their pockets." (*High Tide*, 92) She remembers the kinds of play her mother's acceptance fostered:

> When my mother is canonized, I will testify that she really did sit through a hundred virtually identical productions, staged by my siblings and me, of the play titled approximately "The Dutch Boy Who Saved His Town by Putting His Finger in the Hole in the Dike." I have no idea why we did this. It seems truly obsessive. I can only offer as defense that we had a soft gray blanket with a hole in it, an irresistible prop. We took rave reviews for granted. (92)

In the quiet humor of the anecdote, Kingsolver pays tribute to the wonder of her family's gentle atmosphere, saying later in that same essay, "Raising children is a patient alchemy." (97)

She also recalls the directives of her kindly father. Commenting on his "way of doing things, slow and careful, deliberate and connected," she describes him as the responsible doctor/parent that his profession demanded. She also notes that he "always thought a lot about the consequences of things." (Perry interview, 148) The story that recurs in connection with Dr. Kingsolver is of a road trip from Kentucky to Key West, Florida. Tired of the hot and uncomfortable travel, the three children complained about having nothing to do; the family liked traditional car-travel games, but this trip was longer than usual and longer than expected. Their father's advice was that they occupy themselves in the back seat by counting to a million. They did.

The second strand of the important influence during any person's childhood, according to Kingsolver, is the surrounding of the natural world. Living on a Kentucky farm, she learned the tasks of planting, growing, harvesting, raising animals (including a quantity of pets), and, above all, seeing the way natural processes created life. She wrote about the crucial impact of understanding the natural world in a 2002 essay, in which she questions how "the American childhood" should be measured and privileges what she calls the child

> bred in the back fields and uncultivated edges of America, whose years are measured in genuine, living seasons: The first clear day of winter's end when the maple sap runs; the moment of summer when earth and air have conspired to raise the temperature of a pond so it might embrace the joyous goosebumps of a naked child's skin; the last leaves piled high and leaped upon in autumn; then snowfall, hushed and final as the white endpaper of a favorite book. (Kingsolver and Belt, *Last Stand: America's Virgin Lands*, 11)

She continues beyond the abstract:

> I am one of those lucky ones, whose best memories all contain birdsong and trees. In the long light of summer, on every consecrated Saturday of spring and fall ... my compatriots and I carried out our greatest accomplishments in the company of hickory and maple.... We had no idea we were living at the edge of an epoch.... We knew just enough of our world to eat it alive, swallowing wildness by the mouthful. (13)

Describing "the soft green stems stripped from tall grass stalks, like new asparagus" and "cattail roots and wild onions," Kingsolver brings the reality of those experiences into her reader's sensual imagination.

Having as companions her older brother and younger sister,

much of Kingsolver's memory is of the three children, catching butterflies, helping her father with the bees, collecting the black walnuts that stained their hands and brought on them the derogatory label of "nutter." More pleasantly,

> My brother and sister and I would hoist cane fishing poles over our shoulders, as if we intended to make ourselves useful, and head out to spend a Saturday doing nothing of the kind. We haunted places we called the Crawdad Creek, the Downy Woods (for downy woodpeckers and also for milkweed fluff), and—thrillingly, because we'd once found big bones there—Dead Horse Draw.... We watched birds whose names we didn't know build nests in trees whose names we generally did. We witnessed the unfurling of hickory and oak and maple leaves in the springtime, so tender as to appear nearly edible; we collected them and pressed them with a hot iron under waxed paper when they blushed and dropped in the fall. (*High Tide*, 170–71)

Living in an area of working farms, the Kingsolvers also had animals (raising beef cattle was one source of income). About the problem of children's becoming attached to the livestock, the author remembers, "[W]hen I was a girl growing up among creatures I would someday have to eat, my mother had promised me we would never butcher anything with a first name. Therefore I was always told from the outset which animals I could name." The romance of animals, rather, came from the children's discoveries of large animal bones that could be imagined to be "buffalo, or mastodons." (*Small Wonder*, 121) For the children searching their acres for adventure, the simplest and most natural of props had the biggest benefits. Kingsolver continued,

> We invented the wildest possible stories about what we found. We tried hard (without ever quite succeeding) to get lost, so we might be sorely missed by our parents and perhaps celebrated with funerals we could go back and spy on, as Tom Sawyer did. We packed sandwiches and extra socks and ran away from home forever on the slightest provocation.... We crouched and stalked and

were thrilled by the sight of any wild animal we discovered: Occasionally, we'd catch the black-tipped whisper of a fox sliding through tall weeds. (*Last Stand*, 12)

Memory has the gift of bleaching remote years of boredom or even pain. While she lived her childhood, Barbara Kingsolver was not so easily satisfied with her life on a farm, taking the bus to and from school, wearing mostly hand-me-down clothes rather than new, being excluded from after-school trips for soda and snacks. The house was isolated, "in the middle of an alfalfa field." *Now* a successful writer, she can speak eloquently about her love of nature; she writes "I want wood-thrush poetry. I want mountains." (*Small Wonder*, 36) *Then*, however, writing with some anguish and more self-pity in her diaries, she wished for a more glamorous life—or if not glamorous, more "normal." Above all, she wanted roller skates and, for them, sidewalks.

Born April 8, 1955, in an Annapolis, Maryland, hospital where her father was a staffer during his tour of duty with the U.S. Navy, Barbara was the second of her mother's "ten month" babies. (Rob had been born in Cincinnati, Ohio, where Dr. Kingsolver interned.)

After military service ended, the Kingsolvers returned to the Kentucky counties near their families' home base of Lexington— Dr. Kingsolver wanted to farm as well as practice medicine, and his wife (his sweetheart from junior high school) agreed to such an undertaking. The Kentucky farmland, then, just outside the county seat of Nicholas County, surrounded with acres of alfalfa and tobacco, was Barbara's true home, and she early learned to recognize that some families were poor, some wealthier; and that what happened to the children of those families was often a function of economics. That her father was often paid in baskets and sacks of vegetables rather than in cash or by check also brought home the impact of practical economics. In fact, she recalled later that she felt as if they were poor: "There was never quite enough to go around, and you had to stretch stuff and be concerned about whether the garden will do well." (Perry interview, 148, 152)

Two sets of grandparents living in Lexington made the Kingsolvers' life as a family less dependent on one or the other of the parents, less "nuclear." They had a car; they could go for Sunday dinners; they could enjoy their extended families. From the city life of their maternal grandparents, Nellie and Arthur Raymond Henry, the Kingsolver children knew sidewalks, neatly trimmed lawns, streetlights. But it was from the gardens of the Kingsolver grandparents, Louise Auxier and Roy, that they learned to love sheer bounty: "they had a whole farm packed into a half-acre lot ... [with] fruit trees and flowering trees and chrysanthemums as high as my head," (Beattie, ed., *Kentucky Writers*, 151) Barbara wrote. In this "wonderland" of a garden, their grandmother's flowers were at war with their grandfather's vegetables. From these rich hours and visits evolved Barbara Kingsolver, gardener.

Both sets of grandparents valued hard and productive work, education, and community giving. There were, however, some differences between the families. Descended from working class people, Wendell had put himself through medical school. And although he did not prevent his wife and children from practicing Protestantism, his own belief system may have been closer to a Native American spirituality. Kingsolver writes, "His idea of worship is to sit in a forest and listen to the birds.... [H]e was always driven to serve people who needed him, whether they could pay or not. When I was in grade school we lived in Africa and in the Caribbean for a while. We didn't have very much. In Africa we didn't have running water." (Perry interview, 147–148)

There were things the Kingsolvers did not have in Carlisle, Kentucky, either. When their television set broke, the parents—who didn't like most of what television offered—simply didn't have it repaired. Robert, Barbara, and Ann mostly lived without that component of American culture, though their grandparents had sets, as did their friends. Instead, the Kingsolver home was often filled with music, which Barbara and her siblings absorbed almost effortlessly. Both good musicians, their parents played all types of music, including folk. Wendell played guitar and violin; his wife played piano and mandolin, and sang. They had performed together for years; they liked being included in community functions. After the children were mature enough to play, Rob brought his guitar; Barbara played keyboard, clarinet, and bass clarinet; and Ann, flute and upright bass. While they listened to classical music and jazz, they also relished the Weavers, Pete Seeger, and other folk singers.

All the family members were also readers. Kingsolver remembers the moment when she taught herself to read, staring fixedly at the word *orange*: "I had the idea. It was like Helen Keller; I understood.... [A]ll of a sudden on the exact center of the page there was a word that started with 'o,' and I knew my letters, and I just said the letters, O-R-A-N-G-E. Then, Boing!, 'orange' came into my mind.... That's when I got it, that actually every single one of those words would have a color inside it, or a meaning, or a sense...." (Beattie, ed., 152–53)

She remembers fondly the way her parents made reading into a family activity. In the evening, after a long day of work, all five listened to poems, stories, and even novels, read usually by their father, a man who "reveres books." Sitting in his red leather chair, Wendell Kingsolver read to them things he loved—Dickens, Mark Twain, Robert Burns poems—not limited-vocabulary books written especially for children. In a recent interview, Barbara Kingsolver tells of seeing her father with tears in his eyes as he read a Burns poem. "I was seven, maybe, and my heart stood still, and I understood that words could have more power over people than any sort of physical object. So that, combined with being a social misfit, I think, probably made me a writer." (Beattie, ed., 152)

Kingsolver's theme of seeing herself as some kind of misfit runs through many of her essays and interviews. While her phrasing is strangely negative, the description speaks to her sense of being different from her peers—somewhat isolated in her rural home, dependent on entertaining herself (outside, in the garden, woods, and fields; inside, with books, family games and reading, and her music), and brighter—even more questioning—than most children she knew. (Few of her peers would have read through the encyclopedia as she liked to do.) In some respects, Barbara Kingsolver had a childhood more like that of an earlier-twentieth-century generation, one from the 1930s and early 1940s rather than the 1950s: her life was relatively free from the technological energies let loose by American postwar prosperity. In contrast to a childhood today filled with the busyness of countless scheduled activities, supplemented with a bombardment of electronic games (both hand-held and big-screen), such a modest girlhood provided almost unlimited space and time for exploration. Kingsolver praises her parents for giving her what she calls "a really enriched childhood." "I had parents who gave me books and a love of books," she recalls, "... I really credit my parents for raising me with an eye always to the natural world." (Beattie, ed., 152)

To choose this rural existence was, obviously, the Kingsolvers' attempt to give their children a beginning which was healthy in all respects. The time to learn and the space to explore were to have significant consequences for all three of their children. So too were the genuinely fresh air and the rigorous physical activity of old-fashioned play, of working on the farm, of walking.

The area of Nicholas County itself was not inherently healthful, however. It was dominated by marginal farming and tobacco growing; most farmers were poor. In the town of Carlisle, even though it was the county seat and had a population of only sixteen hundred people, services of all kinds were limited; there was the hospital, the courthouse, the consolidated school. As Kingsolver recalled, the "deeply depressed" Nicholas County harbored many divisions. "There was black and white. There was merchant and farmer. There was a very clear distinction." (Epstein interview, 34) During Barbara's first-grade year, the schools were segregated. Then, in second grade,

> the kids who had gone to school in the CME [Christian Methodist Episcopal] church came down to our school. I remember thinking, 'They must be so scared,' and wanting to ask, but being afraid. Marilyn and Karen were the two African-American kids in my class. I wanted to be friends with them and I didn't know how.... I knew they came from a different world, and I knew that they were outnumbered. (34)

Even though the residents of Carlisle, Kentucky, saw themselves as a tightly knit community, the fabric of friendship was not all-inclusive.

For Barbara, her father's role as doctor to the area and her mother's unflagging participation in the church and other community activities created links that the location of her home might have frustrated. She always understood that *she* was a part of Carlisle; that was one reason for her empathy with the racial outsiders. Her feelings about "small-town life in a rural, agricultural county" are ambivalent: "The best part of that way of life is that everybody knows your business, and the worst part is that everybody knows your business." Still, "friends and neighbors and relatives … will always be there when you need them." (Pence interview, 16)

One of the ways the Kingsolvers resisted being an integral part of the Carlisle mix was to make plans for their children's college educations. Few of Carlisle's children would be college-educated, so Barbara's parents' insistence on academic excellence contributed to her feeling of being different. As much as a child could, she worried about her peers and their futures. Years later she lamented the rates of both illiteracy and college attendance in the state of Kentucky: "It's not just about better-paying jobs—it's about helping kids see the advantage of living more thoughtful, interesting and productive lives." (*Kentucky Monthly*, 13)

It was necessary for the Kingsolvers to supplement the education their children received in the Nicholas County schools. The resources were adequate—though there were no laboratory sciences—but the caliber of instruction was uneven. The children within the school system were of vastly different abilities, which added to the problems of educating them. The system didn't have enough special-area teachers, for example, so all students had to move through reading at the same pace. Barbara, who was an advanced reader, felt punished because when she read fast, her first-grade teacher joked that no one could understand her, and devised an exercise so that the others in her group would call out "stop" whenever she came to a period. Later, in third grade, she and her classmates liked to get their teacher, Miss Marie, "off track"; she told "spellbinding" stories, and if the story went on long enough, they would not get to math.

Seeing Miss Marie's stories as examples of the wealth of oral storytelling in the South, Barbara, shy as she was, also told lots of stories. She was seldom as quiet as her demeanor or her shyness suggested. And she saw much that happened as funny: she later explained that in the South "everything turns into a big colossal whopping tale to amuse each other." (Pence interview, 21) One of her grandfathers used to tell her about planting potatoes on the Kentucky hills that were so steep "you could lop off the ends of rows and let the potatoes roll into a basket." (*High Tide,* 115)

In elementary school, Barbara wrote poems that rhymed; she kept a diary intermittently, a practice she began in second grade; she started piano lessons and practiced diligently and enthusiastically; and she grew. The tallest of her classmates, and among the smartest, she was teased about her string-bean qualities; one of her nicknames was "Queen Sliver." When the boys chased other girls on the playground, she yearned to be popular, too.

But popularity in the economically stratified school went hand in hand with wealth, and the popular kids were the children of merchants and attorneys. They had nice clothes and, later, cars. The farm kids, including the Kingsolvers, were seldom fashionable. Not everyone had indoor plumbing; as Kingsolver remembered, maybe they "didn't get to wash their hair every night because they didn't necessarily have hot water. They had to walk through mud to get to the school bus, so they had mud on their shoes." (Epstein interview, 34) Judging people on appearance alone was anathema to Virginia and Wendell Kingsolver, so they were comfortable dressing their children, at times, in relatives' hand-me-downs. Their attention was on education at its best, and encouraging a child to learn and to be inquisitive was more significant than going on shopping trips to Lexington.

CHAPTER TWO

The World of Experience

We went quite a lot of places. I mean, odd places.
This is not Club Med we're talking about. Just sort
of outlandish, unusual places that were underdevel-
oped or whatever, we went to them.
—Barbara Kingsolver, *Kentucky Writers*

BARBARA KINGSOLVER'S SECURITY as a child depended on her
parents, particularly on her mother. In several memoirs, she recalls
bringing to Virginia all the sweet-pea blossoms she could pick
from a trellis in the yard. The young child notices the "pink red
purple dazzle. A finger painting of colors humming against the
blue air: I could think of nothing but to bring it to you. I climbed
up the wooden trellis and picked the flowers. Every one." (Kingsolver, *I've Always Meant to Tell You*, 251–252) As if to embody the
core of her mother's character, in both accounts Kingsolver has her
mother saying, only, "Thank you, honey" over and over—amid
her tears.

According to the child's memory, one interruption in the placid
stream of this unquestioning love is vacation time, when the Kingsolver parents go off alone and leave Barbara with Grandmother
Henry. Even as the child is thrilled to see her grandmother let
down her hair ("in a silvery waterfall to the back of her knees")

(*Small Wonder*, 161) and to be given special treats, she misses her mother so much—"bitterly"—that she cannot believe her mother can return with a bright smile. Even at three, Barbara wonders whether her mother has missed her:

> On the day of your return I'm standing in the driveway waiting when the station wagon pulls up. You jump out your side, my mother in happy red lipstick and red earrings, pushing back your dark hair from the shoulder of your white sleeveless blouse, turning so your red skirt swirls like a rose with the perfect promise of you emerging from the center. So beautiful.... I understand with a shock that you are extremely happy.... Happy without me. (*Small Wonder*, 161-162)

Another scene Kingsolver recreates is the mournful night of Grandmother Henry's death. Coming in from the porch, where she has been trying to sleep with her siblings during a hot night, she finds her mother awake, in her own deep mourning but ready to comfort the child, who understands that death is permanent. As she folds Barbara into her arms (the mother that is real, the mother "in scent and substance") (163), she explains to the fearful child that Heaven is a mystery—but that "it might be full of beautiful flowers." The child's reverie, then, is of those flowers:

> When I close my eyes I discover it's there, an endless field of flowers. Columbines, blue asters, daisies, sweet peas, zinnias: one single flower bed stretching out for miles in every direction. I am small enough to watch the butterflies come. I know them from the pasture behind our house, the butterflies you taught me to love and name: monarchs, Dianas, tiger swallowtails. I follow their lazy zigzag as they visit every flower, as many flowers as there are stars in the universe. (163–164)

Content to be comforted, Kingsolver trusted both her parents implicitly. She understood that, between them, they knew almost everything.

She also knew even when very young that her parents were not like most of her classmates' families: she accepted their plans to travel (by Pan American jet) to the Congo in Africa (later Zaire, and now Congo again) as an adventure they would have together, as a family. It was the cohesiveness of that unit, and the support of her brother Rob and baby sister Ann, that reassured her. As her parents had presented the plan to their young children, it was exciting. It was meant to be that, as well as "pleasant and happy and adventurous," (Rehm interview) and even if Virginia and Wendell Kingsolver were taken aback at the living conditions, they seldom complained, at least not in front of their children. When the small plane flew over once a month to deliver supplies and medicines, the children raced frantically to find the parachuted parcel. To them, it was an important game; to the Kingsolver parents, it was their only lifeline.

Sent into the territory as part of a physician exchange, Wendell Kingsolver was surprised at the small, windowless concrete-block building that was to serve as his office and operating station. (Wagner-Martin interview) The conditions of the hot, unventilated office forced him to interrupt his work—and, worse, his surgery—to wipe the sweat from his face and to stop the glasses from sliding down his nose. He was also surprised at the tension in the village. Political unrest had already disheartened the Africans; and they were all too conscious that these white-skinned new arrivals might mean more terror. Despite Virginia's friendliness and helpfulness, and the children's readiness to learn the language and to make friends with the African children, the lessons of recent history were impossible to erase. As Virginia Kingsolver recalled, "Things were not running very well." (Annenberg film)

Barbara remembers the other children's suspicion, which centered first on their white skin but then also on her long, dark hair. She recalls that the African children didn't understand that her long hair—she could sit on it—*was* hair. They would try to pull it off. "My mom would explain to me, 'They're not trying to hurt you. They just think you're wearing something weird on your head and they're trying to get you to stop showing off.'" (Epstein interview, 34) Being white-skinned was also perplexing: for the first time in their lives, the Kingsolver children were in the minority position, and made to feel unacceptable by the darker Africans. Kingsolver recently described the discomfort of that time:

> ... [H]ere I was in a place where everyone, everyone around, looked at me as someone who was peculiar and possibly repugnant because of the color of my skin.... [I]nteractions with children were not pleasant ... because they wanted to see what was the matter with me. They would sort of rub my skin to see if the paint would rub off.... (Rehm interview)

The change from the comfort of their Kentucky lives to the dusty deprivation of the Congo was not easy to process. In Carlisle, Barbara had sulked because the expensive horses in the Blue Grass neighborhoods had swimming pools to use for exercise, though no person in Carlisle or its environs had access to such a thing; but now she watched her parents working relentlessly to make what water they could find safe for drinking. (Epstein interview, 34) Nothing in Africa was done without effort. Nothing was clean, and nothing was safe.

For the children, however, possible health dangers—even the spitting cobra on the back step—took second place to the excitement of making new friends. (Wagner-Martin interview, 2003) The three "quickly made our forays out into the village and learned to speak Kituba, which you can do before a certain age.... You can learn another language without knowing it's difficult," (Rehm interview, 1998) Barbara recalled. "Ultimately I got to be good pals with kids who never got over thinking I was pretty ugly but they were benevolent and they played with me anyway...." (Rehm)

One of the wisest observations Kingsolver makes in the process of her emphasizing the benevolence of the African children—accepting as they were of the strange-looking Americans—was that the idea of normality itself was a cultural construct. For the Kingsolver children, who had previously accepted their appearance in the U.S. as "normal," to be found strange, funny, or frightening on the basis of characteristics they had no means of changing was a sobering experience. In many respects, that experience mirrored most of the assumptions they had carried with them to the Congo.

Like most Americans, they had assumed that the material benefits of civilization—the things of their daily lives—were desirable. Yet in this Congolese village, no one had even seen a car. In Barbara's words, "For the first time I faced the possibility that everything I had assumed to be true—how people live, what we assume to be necessary for us to live—things like plumbing or electricity or cars—could be absolutely false, in another place. These were people who did not have plumbing or electricity or cars—or even roads." (Rehm)

There is the awakening of a different moral sense as the Kingsolvers tried to understand, and then accept, the new cultural and spiritual values. The trip itself, so that her father could provide medical treatment for the villagers, was a profound illustration of the Kingsolvers' belief that "money is not the most important thing," that "[t]he most important thing is what you can do for people that will make the world better in some way." (Beattie, ed., 154) Whereas some families might have been so overwhelmed with the physical displacement and the incontrovertible inconvenience that they would not function well, the Kingsolvers saw living in the vastly different African culture as a way to more firmly center themselves.

There is also the exotic side of such an experience. When Barbara and her siblings came home to Carlisle, all their friends were awed by the seeming impossibility of their experience. Barbara noted, somewhat wryly, that "having lived in a place where lions might follow you home from getting the water, doesn't help you fit in, but it also kind of gives you license to see yourself as a little bit different." (154)

For Barbara Kingsolver the writer, Africa remains firmly linked to writing. She often tells the story of her beginning to keep a journal in conjunction with the trip to Africa, a journal which begins with her first glimpse of the terrain from the plane window. "When I first saw Africa," she wrote, "I thought it was a cloud." (*High Tide*, 119) A wonderful sentence in its suggestiveness, it becomes a kind of linchpin for the child's coming to understand the power of words—especially the power of metaphor. In a related and not simply explanatory sentence, Kingsolver later notes, "It takes time to peer through the vapor and understand." (120)

Becoming a writer, for Kingsolver, was a long and almost halting process. But she focuses back to this moment when she caught the mystifying experience in one sentence. Usually, after she quotes the line, she discusses the years of her subsequent journal keeping: "I have just a whole drawer-full of those little dumb diaries in my office in Tucson, and then I have a whole bookshelf of spiral-bound notebooks." (Beattie, ed., 154) The point is, however, that Kingsolver wrote so much because she early understood that "writing is the thing that makes the experience real to me." (154)

The impression those months in Africa made on the second-grader is clear: she began a novel about postcolonial Africa in the 1990s, after ten years away. The book's substance is the life of Africa in the early 1960s under political torment, but the narrative is more readily about the Kingsolvers' story—father, mother, and three children in real life, transmuted to father, mother, and four children in *The Poisonwood Bible*.

Knowing the African culture and some of its language when she was a child gave Kingsolver the ability to create the myriad of details that gave the novel a sense of authenticity. The experience was more factually accurate than it was emotionally true, however, because the Kingsolver parents were vastly different from their fictional counterparts, the Prices. In the acknowledgments to the novel, Kingsolver thanks her parents "for being different in every way from the parents I created for the narrators of this tale. I was the fortunate child of medical and public-health workers, whose compassion and curiosity led them to the Congo. They brought me to a place of wonders, taught me to pay attention, and set me early on a path of exploring the great, shifting terrain between righteousness and what's right." (Kingsolver, *Poisonwood Bible*, x)

Safely back in Carlisle, first by the delivery plane and then by jet, the Kingsolvers were all in need of a reorientation. Hard as everyone worked, life in the States was so much more comfortable—and safer—than it had been in the Congo that being in Kentucky made them euphoric. They followed the news of the supposedly independent Congo with great sorrow.

To respond to Barbara's constant badgering that she be given piano lessons, her mother found a piano teacher in Carlisle, and the child made rapid (if rough) progress. Barbara was practicing harder and harder pieces—and she practiced, it seemed, all the time. There was little doubt that music would become a "huge part" of her existence. (Wagner-Martin interview)

The Kingsolvers settled back into their Kentucky routines, living through rainy seasons and droughts, selling one year's crops and planting the next, watching their children learn and grow, spending more and more time helping to care for their respective parents in Lexington. Dr. Kingsolver could see that if they were to go on another medical mission, it should be soon—before any of their parents became entirely dependent, and before any of their children refused to leave friends and school.

So when Rob was in ninth grade, Barbara in seventh, and Ann in second, the Kingsolvers found themselves living in the very simple accommodations of a convent on the island of St. Lucia in the Lesser Antilles. Dr. Kingsolver's office and hospital were also in the convent. The several months that they spent in the Caribbean Islands marked another memorable period: enforced time together made them appreciate the love within their family at a time when many adolescents were turning their backs on parents and siblings. The St. Lucian culture was as captivatingly beautiful as the African had been, but not so threatening politically. Again, Dr. Kingsolver delivered a great many babies, many of them difficult and dangerous births.

Back in Carlisle, Barbara carefully put away her journals and diaries and went back to practicing the clarinet, which she had chosen as her instrument for band, and the piano. She found herself, literally, taken in hand one afternoon by a substitute music teacher, who asked her to come upstairs into the attic where there was a good piano. (Wagner-Martin interview) Well-trained as a pianist herself, the teacher knew how scarce resources for promising young musicians were in Carlisle. She corrected Barbara's technique; gave her music by Chopin, Bach, and Brahms; and met with her weekly in the attic. By challenging her to perform more difficult compositions—the work of famous musicians—this thoughtful teacher came into Barbara's life at a crucial time. Throughout her high school years that followed, the Kingsolvers drove Barbara to Lexington weekly, so that she could study with conservatory-trained teachers.

To the talented, self-motivated Barbara, high school seemed to be just four years to endure before she could once more leave Carlisle—this time for college, and on her own. The school, like the town, was too small. There was nothing appealing for her to think of doing; in fact, the attitudes of Carlisle led her to pretend she was "dumber" than she was, and she continued to complain about her clothes, her hair, her body. (*High Tide*, 41) By sixth grade, she was already five feet, nine inches tall; but she would be a senior in high school before she weighed a hundred pounds. (81)

Kingsolver wrote recently that her high-school diaries were records of what she perceived as failures: on the personal side, she found herself "too tall and shy to be interesting to boys. Too bookish." More generally, "I wrote poems and songs, then tore them up after unfavorable comparison with the work of Robert Frost or Paul Simon. My journal entries were full of a weirdly cheerful brand of self-loathing. 'Dumb me' was how I christened any failure, regardless of its source." (*Small Wonder*, 145)

For someone eager to by-pass the years required in Nicholas county High School, however, Kingsolver plunged in to what the school had to offer. She joined the French Club and the Library Club; the Pep Club (the athletic boosters' group); the Speech Club, which was also the conduit to the Thespians; and not only the band and the marching band but also the stage band, which most years was a jazz group. (Annenberg film) Her grades in classes were A's once again, so as soon as an initiation was held for her class, she became a member of the National Honor Society. By her senior year, she was president of both the French Club and the Library Club.

The shadows memory casts are pervasive, however. In the same essay, Kingsolver wrote, "Turning page after page in those old cardboard-bound diaries now, reading the faint penciled entries (I lacked even the confidence to use a pen), I dimly grasp in my memory the bleakness of that time. I feel such sadness now for that girl...." (*Small Wonder*, 146) She had in an earlier essay connected her misery then with one of her abilities now as a writer:

> I gained things from my rocky school years: A fierce wish to look inside of people. An aptitude for listening. The habit of my own company. The companionship of keeping a diary, in which I gossiped, fantasized, and invented myself.... I explored the psychology of the underdog, the one who can't be what others desire but who might still learn to chart her own hopes. (*High Tide*, 42)

In fact, she was an exceptional student who began high school by winning a state-wide essay contest, closed it out as valedictorian of her class, and played Edvard Grieg's Concerto in A Minor at the school's graduation ceremony. (Wagner-Martin interview) During those four years, her teachers worried only that they could not keep her interested; they found extra projects, and extra responsibilities, for her. Yet in her journals, as she admits, she often called herself *stupid*.

Kingsolver's involvement with music created an alternate life for her. It took her into new depths of her own concentration and ability, but it also took her outside Carlisle—to Lexington, for the piano lessons that were so necessary; to area and state music contests, where she met other high-school students who were as entrenched in the love of, and practice of, the piano as she; and eventually to college, where her acceptance, and her funding, depended in part on her skill as a pianist. The hours of daily practice were subsumed by her busy schedule because she wanted to do this work: whereas she also practiced clarinet and bass clarinet, those hours were never so important nor so passionate. The challenge of finding a piece by Liszt or Beethoven that she could master, drawn partly from the music she had heard at home—

either from the classical music stations or from recordings—was a means of pitting herself and her developing abilities against the lesser world that Carlisle represented. (Wagner-Martin interview)

Through the area and state piano competitions, too, Kingsolver came to meet her first boyfriend. Set in contrast to her classmates at Nicholas County High School, this talented musician—who, like her, was headed for a good college—was the first compatible male she had found herself drawn to. For those same reasons, she liked being a part of the stage band, where the boys who were talented musically were also her good friends.

Working on the farm was another good corrective to the apparent anxiety she felt during some periods of high school. In season, she knew that she could excel at picking tent caterpillars off the apple trees and disposing of them in a gasoline fire. Her father paid her a penny for each. And she was proud of finally getting strong enough to hoist a bale of hay into the wagon, rather than having to drive the tractor because she could not handle the heavier work. (*High Tide*, 243)

Nature remained a solace for her. She still found time to be outdoors:

> I remember lying on my back in summertime, staring skywards through the leaves with my head resting on woody roots that were the bunioned feet of a particular old maple.... [C]louds and birds slipped through the blue spaces between leaves as I looked up through them for what seemed to be hours, or magically concentrated years. (*Last Stand*, 13–14)

But the wonderfully interesting outdoors had, with the years, paled. Rob was busy with after-school jobs, and he focused his life on getting his learner's permit and then his driver's license—and eventually his own second-hand car. It was hard for him to make time for hikes with his sisters, though Barbara recalls their paw-paw hunting and feasting. She reminisces about eating her "first—and hundredth—wild pawpaw, a fruit few people have tasted because it can't be transported, only pulled from the branch and licked from the fingers like a handful of rich, banana-scented custard." (*Last Stand*, 12)

High school demanded cars. People went places, even if it was only to drive around the small towns or to stop at a rootbeer stand or a Dairy Queen. Kingsolver's "flunking" her driving test the spring that she turned sixteen was another failure she considered major. She describes herself as "rigid with panic" (*High Tide*, 103) while driving Rob's Volkswagen Beetle: "I rolled backward precariously while starting on a hill; I misidentified in writing the shape of a railroad crossing sign." It was another of her "stupid" acts.

In her mind, the car culture symbolized sexual activity—identified as positive in her imagination. She so wanted to be someone boys would date. She describes her first kiss—at band camp, when she was fourteen—and uses the experience to warn her daughter about trying too hard to please a boy. ("It took me years to get over being flattered and flattened by any kind of male approval.") (*Small Wonder*, 152) More usually, Kingsolver saw the car culture as a means of trapping the girls of Nicholas County—once pregnant, they would never go to professional school or college; they might never marry, or they would marry quickly. In Kingsolver's best acidic tone, she writes, "[I]t was rugged going to high school in a place where the only things available for teenagers to do in the way of entertainment took place in the back seat of a car, or the front seat, if you were a boy and liked to drag race. That was it." (Beattie, ed., 155)

Life in Nicholas County was determined chiefly by gender. Boys could drag race; girls had to "neck" and "pet." Boys could hold jobs that paid decently; girls clerked or waitressed or cleaned houses or picked apples. Even a young Barbara recognized inequities; barely in her teens, she proselytized to her mother about women's life choices. At thirteen, "a tempest of skinned knees and menarche," while learning to bleach laundry, she confronted her mother: "Just one thing.... Name one good thing about being a woman...." (*Small Wonder*, 164) Setting up her honest, and always beloved, mother, who—busy with the piles of wash—doesn't think as fast as normal, she prods her further; and when her mother replies vaguely that "[t]here are lots of good things," Barbara repeats, "Just name me one." In her mother's hesitation, she feels victorious: "[B]ecause you'd hesitated I knew I didn't have to believe it." (Her mother's answer had been "the love of a man.")

Most of Kingsolver's romances during high school came from her reading—novels and non-fiction, stories in magazines, books for adolescents as well as adult readers. She haunted the Bookmobile; she was a regular at the public library. She mingled children's classics like Robert Louis Stevenson's *Treasure Island* with classics for girls like Louisa May Alcott's *Little Women*. Of the four sisters in *Little Women*, Kingsolver liked Jo the best—not because Jo wanted to become a writer, but because Jo was a "tomboy," a role that Kingsolver found appealing. (Perry interview, 149)

On her own, she found Margaret Mitchell's *Gone with the Wind* (a novel that was "not what I expected") (*High Tide*, 50), Dostoyevsky's *Crime and Punishment*, and other Russian novels; from her childhood she had read Charles Dickens, and more recently, she drank in the ironic humor of Barbara Pym's social comedy. (60) But it was Miss Truman Richey's suggestion during her junior year of school that Barbara learn the Dewey Decimal System, and in doing that, recatalogue all the books in the high-school library, that allowed Kingsolver to find other worlds of reading. (50)

One of the first writers she grew excited over was William Saroyan, when she found his *The Human Comedy* wrongly shelved among books on human anatomy. She took the novel home and read it voraciously. (Annenberg film) Another was Doris Lessing, whose Martha Quest became a kind of role model. She loved the narratives of Africa, as well as Lessing's focus on women's lives—and felt that she had come to prefer books that were about "something important" rather than just escape. (Perry interview, 150) From Lessing, she found Nadine Gordimer and then the quietly evocative Virginia Woolf, with her poetic "woman's sentence" and narratives about women's daily lives—but, unlike Jane Austen, not always women's lives subordinated to men's lives. (*Small Wonder*, 153) The writings by Woolf and Lessing proved that women's stories could *be* art: they could fascinate readers if, somehow, they were told well enough.

When Miss Richey gave Kingsolver the long assignment of mastering Dewey Decimal, and along the way unearthing countless writers that were unfamiliar to her, she gave the teenager a way out of her social dilemma. Barbara now had work to do, important work. She no longer had empty hours to lament that no boy from the Violators motorcycle gang knew who she was, that she often was given her cousin's unstylish clothes, that she wore "black lace-up oxfords" and had recently been introduced to the cafeteria line as "The Bride of Frankenstein." (*High Tide*, 48, 55) Miss Richey may have saved Kingsolver's last years of high school, in fact, because these newly discovered books led her to "nothing short of a complete transformation, the kind of soul-shattering revelation that some people find in religious salvation." (*Small Wonder*, 153)

In her identification with the women characters in the fiction of Lessing, as well as Margaret Drabble and Marilyn French, she recalls, "These writers put names to the kind of pain I'd been feeling for so long, the ways I felt useless in a culture in which women could be stewardesses but the pilots were all men. They helped me understand why I'd been so driven by the opinions of men." (153)

The process was just beginning in high school, however. Kingsolver still longed to be cute, to wear smart clothes (and made for herself—in her years of home economics classes—"an applegreen polyester jumpsuit [which was] supremely fashionable for about two months") (*High Tide*, 55), and above all, to wear enough make-up to appear glamorous. In a journal entry dating to when she was fifteen, she rages at her mother for her overprotectiveness ("without courage or any real intention, yet, of actually revealing myself to you"): "Why do you want to ruin my life? Why can't you believe I know how to make my own decisions? Why do you treat me like a child? No makeup or nail polish allowed in this house— you must think I am a baby or a nun...." (*Small Wonder*, 164–165) In her retrospective commentary, Kingsolver adds, "I am a young woman sliced in two, half of me claiming to know everything and the other half just as sure I will never know anything at all. I am too awkward and quiet behind my curtain of waist-length hair, a girl unnoticed, a straight-A schoolmouse who can't pass for dumb and cute in a small-town, marry-young market that values—as far as I can see—no other type." (165)

As she wrote later in "Letter to a Daughter at Thirteen," she feels such pain for this girl. Yet Kingsolver also knew that her new reading material was intensifying her adolescent differences from her caring parents. She writes about the "danger" of some books, especially those by Lessing:

> [T]hey will broaden our experience and blend us more deeply with our fellow humans. Sometimes this makes waves. It made some at my house. We had a few rocky years while I sorted out new information about the human comedy, the human tragedy, and the ways some people are held to the ground unfairly. I informed my parents that I had invented a new notion called *justice*.... (*High Tide*, 51)

Aggressively intellectual in some ways, Kingsolver as a writer was not making the same kinds of waves. She had learned to write poems in free forms, but their subjects were still somewhat self-serving and didactic; she describes them as "earnest and frequently whiny." (*Small Wonder*, 231) More significantly, her adolescent fiction was about men and boys on adventures; "the protagonists of these stories were always boys." (*High Tide*, 250) The stories she wrote differed from those she read.

During these years of undiluted As and, more important, her enjoyment of all her classes—English, history, geometry and advanced algebra, French, biology, chemistry, music—Kingsolver felt that she was waging a running battle with herself as her family's daughter. In an apologetically comic voice, she describes the life of "skinny, unsought-after girls" (*High Tide*, 48) as being that of "cutting up in class, pretending to be surly, and making up shocking, entirely untrue stories about my home life. I wonder now that my parents continued to feed me." In a more serious tone, she recognizes that her mother's frustration with her tendency to belittle herself was justified. (*Small Wonder*, 146)

Along with her escapes into nature and into books, Kingsolver's music was the third area of involvement she found increasingly useful as a distraction from leading her typically adolescent, small-town life. As she learned more and more difficult compositions, she enjoyed the sheer labor of practicing—developing the muscles in her hands and fingers; learning to use her physical power for more effective intervals, grace notes, glissandos; working out better fingering; memorizing, memorizing, memorizing. Although she was never considered to be an actual piano prodigy, Barbara was both diligent and talented. She practiced hard and regularly, and she was blessed with a general musicianship that allowed her to play with nuance. She received "superior" ratings in competition. The tall, willowy girl bent intently over the keyboard impressed listeners with her expert, and often moving, renditions of Bach, Chopin, Beethoven.

It was her talent as a pianist that won Kingsolver a music scholarship at DePauw University. That Indiana school had attracted her because she was interested in going to a good liberal-arts school with an excellent reputation in both music and academics. (She also wanted to be far enough away from home that she could return for most holidays but not every weekend.) When she visited the campus in Greencastle, she mentioned the various fields she might major in, music being one. Spontaneously, the interview team asked if she would like to audition for them. (Wagner-Martin interview) Confident from doing well at a state contest with a Bach and Gershwin program, she played. After some consultation outside the hall, the committee offered her a music performance scholarship. She looked no further for the place to spend her college years.

CHAPTER THREE

The Worlds of Indiana, Europe, and Arizona

I found bonds of friendship that had to do with common interests and sort of the joy of shared intellectual discovery, and that was nice.... I didn't have to be embarrassed about having a life and a mind.

—Barbara Kingsolver, *Kentucky Writers*

IT WAS NEVER AS IF Barbara Kingsolver wanted terribly to leave Carlisle, Kentucky. What she wanted was a way to find her autonomy. Even if she already had some idea of who she was, a girl with many talents and skills, she felt continually overshadowed as an individual by her family, a unit that was unbelievably good, moral, and giving. Living up to the values and work ethic of her parents was itself a tough aim. And she had not yet done any of the kind of living she thought might be ahead for her, her father's daughter. Dr. Kingsolver was, after all, a man blessed with "the spirit of wild adventure, and in the most challenging circumstances." (Wagner-Martin interview)

The summer before her senior year at Nicholas County High, she had lived with her grandparents in Lexington and enrolled in music classes at University of Kentucky; she had her first taste of both music theory and music history, and found the actual study of music fascinating. She also met some boys, and she learned that what she thought of as her unfashionable height would not always alienate people. She also learned that it was all right to be smart, talented, or both. The summer-school experience sent her into her senior year with a slightly more positive outlook, and made her plans for leaving for college even more intriguing.

But now that the summer after graduation was ending, and she was getting a roomful of books, music, clothes, and other paraphernalia ready to make the trip three hundred miles northwest, to the campus of DePauw University, she was filled with impatience: she wanted to leave. She wanted to become a college woman. She was, as she recalled, "thrilled to the edge of all my senses to be starting college." (*Small Wonder*, 165)

The drive over was quiet. And after her parents left in their Volkswagen bus, and before her roommates had appeared, to her surprise Kingsolver felt the most desperate and tormenting loneliness. Tears slick on her cheeks, she realized that three hundred miles was as frighteningly distant as being a continent away. She knew nobody at DePauw. She was going to miss the family she had yearned to leave behind.

In the dormitory corridors, institutional green paint backed the numerous unfamiliar faces of first-year students—women in one building, men in another. Out of the mass, the tall, thin Barbara Kingsolver was memorable, her pleasant face animated, smiling, a little hesitant.

She found herself reassured about this college business. Organized, she went to class on time; she had the right notebook, and she had read the assignment. She ate her meals when food service was open. She used the shower early. College was manageable. Any leftover time she spent on her music in a tiny, cell-like practice room in the music building. That building quickly became her home away from the dormitory room. She needed to spend long hours there, and in lessons and with the orchestra, where she had moved from clarinet to bassoon, undertaking an entirely new kind of study. In order to be a part of the early music groups that played in local coffee houses, she learned to play the recorder; she also accompanied soloists and groups—she seldom declined a request.

Among the students who were music majors she found a new family. (Wagner-Martin interview) They all carried impossible schedules of classes, lessons, and practice times. They had little time to meet people who were not music students; besides, what interested them, individually and collectively, was music.

They walked to classes together, ate lunch together, encouraged one another in the practice rooms. They complained about the amount of work they needed to do, but they were all so talented that they made rapid progress. High achievers, they saw before them hushed stages with thousands of people rapt in the audience, recording contracts, careers that meant learning more and more, practicing more and more great compositions—and perhaps writing and orchestrating some of their own.

For Kingsolver, however, the quantities of time that her music and its practice demanded began to seem oppressive. She let the question of who would really succeed as a performer enter her thoughts—there were not many slots in the concert world for new, young artists. And she had never intended to become a music teacher, although the music concentration demanded that she become proficient in one instrument from each of the four classical groups. She saw years of continued study ahead. She saw even more years of competition. And she found herself surrounded by a number of young musicians who were already superior to her, both in ability and in training.

Kingsolver's curiosity led her to meet a number of freshmen (other than her group of music-major friends) who were as excited as she about the chance to learn new things and to share new ideas. She was one of the women in pajamas talking after hours in the lounge. She remembered what a revelation it all was:

I had spent so much time being sort of secretive and embarrassed about who I was because of not fitting in, and then when I went to college, well, I got a lot happier ... because, lo and behold, I found other people who liked to read books.

(Beattie, ed., 155–156)

She discovered Karl Marx and, to her surprise, understood the concept of class struggle from her experiences in Carlisle, Kentucky. "I know this stuff. I grew up with this stuff.... [Kentucky is] a laboratory of class consciousness because you have really oppressed workers shoulder to shoulder with big capital [and] mining bosses who sort of own their workers wholesale." (Epstein interview, 34)

It was the early 1970s. She found the politics of antiwar protests, and with a quantity of other DePauw students, marched on campus to end the Vietnam conflicts; she found equally disgusting the inequities faced by Spanish-speaking farm laborers in the prosperous Indiana midlands, and worked as a volunteer to help better the conditions of the transient families. (*Small Wonder,* 154) Having political convictions is "not an abstract thing," she would say later. (Pence interview, 14) "I just happen to live in a world that has things like child abuse, unfair immigration policies, environmental disaster and racism and sexism as a part of daily life." She was amazed that a good number of her DePauw friends felt just as she did.

Already thinking of herself as a feminist, already impatient with the married women of her parents' generation for succumbing to the conventions of the good wife—giving up all their dreams and ambitions to run a household—she read well beyond Betty Friedan's *The Feminine Mystique* (1963). She agreed with Friedan that the repression of a woman's talent was the root of the "problem that had no name"; she read Germaine Greer, Robin Morgan, Gloria Steinem, and the new magazine *Ms.* Barbara Kingsolver would *be* a "Ms." She might never marry. But if she did, *his* name would not automatically become *hers.*

Some of these writers she had found in high school, but now at DePauw, she "really sank into them, reading the way a drowning person breathes air when she finally breaks the surface." (*Small Wonder,* 153–154) She later recalled, "I stayed up late reading; I sat all day in the library on Saturdays, reading. Every word made sense to me, every claim brought me closer to being a friend to myself.... [T]hese writers allowed me to imagine other possibilities." The scales fell rapidly from her eyes.

While Kingsolver did not need to change her name or her

wardrobe on the surprisingly eclectic Midwestern campus, she did need to change her speech. Not that any of the Kingsolvers or their circle of friends had ever used incorrect grammar; no, the problem was that Barbara Kingsolver, the tall woman with the unique surname, had an accent—a softly Southern accent, not unpleasant to hear, but a marker that, for the early 1970s, was unfashionable. The stereotypical picture of the South was that everyone there was lazy: no one got work done; no one finished the ending of words. She recalls complete strangers stopping her on campus and asking her to pronounce the words "oil" and "hair." (Beattie, ed., 156) She decided that there were some traits she had no control over; her speech, however, was within her power. She eliminated her Kentucky accent.

She also rid herself of her long and somewhat childlike dark hair. And when she returned from the Christmas holidays, she wore a green pith helmet (from the Kingsolver storage attic) with an army surplus overcoat she had bought to protect herself from the rains and snows of central Indiana. Wearing the ankle-length coat with its bulky zip-out lining, she "became a known figure on campus ... [and her] social life picked right up." (*High Tide*, 56)

Anger had replaced timidity, or what Kingsolver called her "chameleon" quality (Beattie, ed., 156); and she made change after change. She dressed for "function rather than sexiness" (*Small Wonder*, 154); she "joined a women's group on campus, then found a church that was more forgiving of personal lapses of judgment than of larger, social ones, such as war and hunger." She dated, went to a few bars, and had "a genuine social life" (167) even as she later realized that the euphoria and rebellion of being free from an overprotective home might have blurred her judgment. At least, she survived her freshman year.

When Kingsolver returned as a sophomore, she lived off campus. She kept the money-making jobs (cleaning houses, learning typesetting) from her freshman year and added a new way to earn money, the $5-an-hour modeling for artists. (Wagner-Martin interview) She saw her friends. She stayed a music major for the fall semester. But with her decision to change majors from music to biology began a series of efforts that would make her eventual transfer to science possible. She didn't want to leave the world of music, but she feared not making it as a concert pianist; yet she didn't want to give up the DePauw Junior Year Abroad program. Her problem was to take enough biology courses to complete that major in the next several years, even while being abroad. Above all, she didn't want to lose her scholarship funding.

The plan she devised showed her ingenuity, as well as her ability to work independently. She had had no biology courses, nor had she taken any classes that had laboratory components. Nevertheless, she studied all the textbooks for the series of introductory science courses; then she sat for exams in each. (Wagner-Martin interview) Because she passed this preliminary coursework, she began the science curriculum in the second semester of her sophomore year with an upper level laboratory course in organic chemistry. She did well; she was given junior status, and her scholarship was transferred from the conservatory to academic programs. She still had funding.

Kingsolver found several fine science professors who helped her discover and study additional work. Dr. Preston Adams, in particular, treated her as if she were one of the graduate students. She came to love biology: "I think biology is my religion. Understanding the processes of the natural world and how all living things are related." (Perry interview, 147) Introduced to the work of E.O. Wilson by Professor Adams, Kingsolver had an eye on the then-emerging field of kinship study in ecology.

She relinquished the music major, too, because she was felt it limiting, and she was hungry to take other courses (Wagner-Martin interview)—"East Asian history and anthropology and psychology and computer sciences and math and physics and chemistry," (Beattie, ed., 156) as well as literature courses and one class in creative writing. Here she began what would become a decade of work on the short story "Homeland." The move from her acquisitive process through information—learning whatever came before her—to a stance more like her capacity in music, to make that learning her own, was difficult to achieve with writing. So much a person who absorbed knowledge, Kingsolver had been rewarded for those abilities throughout her life. To learn to pause and transform that knowledge into something new, something her own, would take time.

The story when she wrote it for the writing class at DePauw was titled "The Last Remaining Buffalo East of the Mississippi." It was a visualization of the way a Native American woman living in the white culture of the Midwest would feel after all her traditional values had been stripped of their meaning. True to the plot of what became "Homeland," when the great-grandmother's family takes her back to her birthplace—a town called Cherokee—and she fails to recognize the place, one of the commercialized, tawdry exhibits in the tourist trap is "the last buffalo." What Kingsolver eventually does with the poignant story is draw Great Mam, who smokes her pipe on the front porch in the evenings, as a wise survivor who—in a chary, non-emotional language—passes a great amount of her Indian heritage to her eleven-year-old great-granddaughter, whom she has named Waterbug. Woven through the legends and lore, the story has the resonance of legend itself. It is also a story of a great love between a girl and a woman from disparate generations.

Kingsolver recounts that she had long been fascinated by her father's Cherokee great-grandmother and wondered what her life in the hill country of Kentucky, where the fact that one had Native American blood would be repressed, had been like. Starting with the "Last Buffalo" version which she wrote at nineteen, Kingsolver admitted, "I rewrote that story every single year." (Perry interview, 158) She never felt it was right.

She finally realized that its treatment was too autobiographical—too full of "junk that's in there just because it really happened"—so she made radical changes. First, "I went to the library and read nothing but Cherokee legends.... Then I went back and wrote the sentence, 'My great-grandmother belonged to the Bird Clan.' And I kept that high note all through the story." (158)

Giving the story this legendary tone, making it "more distant," was one of Kingsolver's first attempts to control the *way* something was said or written. She was learning that "story" is not only event or character, but a work of words.

In that knowledge came as well her sense that the writer has a mission, often to save words—and events and characters—that would otherwise fall into oblivion. In an interview, she said, "I feel 'Homeland' expresses my reason for being as a writer. I hope that story tells about the burden and the joy and the responsibility of holding on to the voices that are getting lost. That's what I want to do as a writer." (158)

Other pieces of writing that came from her second year in college had to do with her trying to express her catastrophic violation after a man she had met in a bar a few days earlier showed up at her door, forced his way in, and raped her. In the shame of that episode—shame because she knew her parents would not have approved her going to bars, encouraging people she met there, or opening her door to a near stranger—she could for a time do nothing but withdraw. When she later wrote about the experience in "A Letter to My Mother," she pictured herself "curled like a fetus on my bed. Curling in a knot so small I hope I may disappear. I do not want to be alive." (*Small Wonder*, 167) But in this prose-poem meditation, written many years after the horror of the rape (a horror that time does not diminish), she also writes, "I will be able to get up from this bed only if I can get up angry." (168)

In 1974, there was no such term as "acquaintance rape." There was no way the college woman could have reported her attacker, even though she knew his name and would no doubt have to see him on campus. The legal system barely acknowledged any forced intercourse as "rape," so until some language was invented, Kingsolver was left to her own despair. In a later poem, "This House I Cannot Leave," she images that despair—and the pervasive and long-lasting sadness of it—as she writes to comfort a friend whose house has been robbed. The poem opens, "My friend describes the burglar," and it continues through the friend's sense of violation after the act. She must sell, she must leave behind her newly painted walls, her garden, her fruit trees; she must rid herself of his desecration. The poem pauses as the poet–speaker identifies with her grief: "[T]he trees have stopped growing for her." The moment of turn in the poem, as Kingsolver takes the reader to her own "robbery," her body as house, is still imaged in the literal house and land. The poem ends,

> I offer no advice.
> I tell her I know, she will leave. I am thinking
> of the man who broke and entered
>
> me.
> Of the years it took to be home again
> in this house I cannot leave.
>
> (Kingsolver, *Another America/Otra America*, 37)

Leaving Greencastle, Indiana, then, may have been a way to start over—as well as a way to satisfy Kingsolver's ever-increasing wanderlust. More like her father than she had realized, the simple act of moving to new terrain, surrounding herself with unknown people and then making a place for herself, became a definition of the power of self. She, Barbara Kingsolver, could accomplish all these things. In autumn of 1975, she traveled to Greece, where she was enrolled at the Hellenic-American Union in Athens, the best program for her—partly because she could take a science course that would work toward her major requirements at DePauw. (Wagner-Martin interview) Classes at the Union took up only four days a week, so every weekend she hitchhiked. One weekend, she got as far as Rome, trusting to the drivers of whatever vehicles she ended up in to convey her safely, and with interest. Although she was not taping any of their conversations, she was hungrily listening.

Kingsolver was fascinated with her life. She did not want to go home. In order to stay through the spring semester, she applied for a vocational permit, to work as an archaeological assistant, and on that work permit she went to France. There she helped with a Neolithic dig; later, there were openings for personnel at a medieval dig in England. There she dug a well. But she preferred France and, during the summer, found an apartment to sublet in Paris.

Besides the digs, Kingsolver worked as an artist's model at the Sorbonne, cleaned houses and apartments, did some translating, and found work as a typesetter. (Wagner-Martin) Busy but exhilarated with her new experiences, she tried to find ways to finish her degree from abroad. She saw herself as a perpetual rolling stone, and her parents tactfully didn't object. The freedom of being away from the United States culture, which she had come to understand all too well after twenty years of living in it, was an immense part of her attraction to other countries and other customs. But just as strong an attraction was the fact that these cultures offered so much that she would never understand—unless she lived within them. In a kind of definitive understatement, Kingsolver said recently that she simply "loved living abroad." (Wagner-Martin)

Referring to these months as her "rolling stone" period, she admitted that she learned a great many things that even a liberal-arts college could not certify or accept. So finally, she had to return to DePauw to finish her requirements. Carrying a heavy course-load, she graduated with her class, in the spring of 1977; because her grade-point average was over 3.7, she was awarded the degree *magna cum laude*. Nothing less than phenomenal, Kingsolver's record at the small college—including all the credits lost when she changed from the conservatory to the biology major—made her a memorable student for the teachers who had known her.

After spring graduation, she returned immediately to France. She spent some time in Greece again as well, but most of the employment she found placed her in France, fast becoming the country of her heart. Eventually, however, since she was a U.S. citizen, even all her work capabilities could not keep the work visa renewed. Her brother's wedding served as a good event to bring her home, and once back in Carlisle, she felt even more strongly that she could not make Kentucky—or Greencastle, Indiana—her professional location.

Gathering her resources, buying a used "tiny yellow Renault," (*High Tide*, 6) and collecting what information she could, Kingsolver "drove with all [she] owned" for Arizona. She had almost no contacts there; she had no employment awaiting her; she had nothing but the same kind of resolve that had led her successfully through Europe. How hard could it be to try a different part of the United States? They spoke English in Arizona, after all.

The haunting qualities of the Southwest drew her—native cultures, stark beauty, unusual plants and flowers. She described the region in her introduction to *Southwest Stories*: "the Southwest: a prickly land where bears make bets with rabbits, and the rabbits win. Where nature rubs belly to belly with subdivision and barrio, and coyotes take short cuts through the back alley." (Kingsolver, 3) The mixed population, each segment complete with its customs; the strangely beautiful terrain; the unfamiliar animals—Kingsolver the biologist and anthropologist was attracted. While she didn't think she would stay permanently in Arizona, it was another of the places she wanted to experience. Still a rolling stone, she described herself as "a typical young American, striking out[,] ... the commonest kind of North American refugee." (*High Tide*, 6)

She had virtually no money, so she rented what she came to see as "a horrible apartment" in downtown Tucson. But she soon landed an unbelievably good job in the University of Arizona Medical School Physiology Department as a medical technician. Beyond her expectations of a transient kind of job, this one paid reasonably well and had medical benefits. Her supervisors gave her a lot of responsibility; it was an interesting job; and before long, she had enough money saved to rent a house, her first house, in a better part of town. (Wagner-Martin interview) By that time she had come to know the Spanish-speaking culture, and she was beginning to see the Native American influence. And she also had found the Sanctuary movement.

CHAPTER FOUR

Arizona Lives

I began writing stories about the people behind the picket fence with the paint peeling off it. The people who have lunch down at the Talk of the Town Restaurant.... The people who drive too fast on Scrubgrass Road. The people who have never thought themselves worth very much, but whose lives are full of not just quiet desperation, but a lot of joyful moments.
                              —Barbara Kingsolver, *Kentucky Writers*

FINDING A GROUP who worked with the Sanctuary refugees gave Kingsolver the kind of passionate involvement she had missed once she returned to Carlisle from Europe. Different as her housemates in France had been—"talkative French socialists and a few British expatriates" (*Small Wonder*, 168)—they had shared a willingness to be identified with commitment. Once Kingsolver had lived even a few weeks in her tranquil home in Kentucky, she restlessly missed her outspoken friends, people—like herself—"at some loose coupling in our lives between school and adulthood," (168) their evenings filled with "a happy, pointless argument about Camus," (169) for example. They had not yet had to make the expected choices, the capitulation to the routine in both philosophy and life, which—they feared—could only deaden their imaginations.

The heady freedom that Kingsolver equates with her time in Europe was not entirely geographical or cultural. By virtue of her own age and education, she was surrounded with people who shared her interests—the intellectuals of her generation, whether Greek or British or German or French. One of the qualities that Tucson offered was this mix of well-educated (or at least curious) youth; Kingsolver refers to the city as "kind of like a big, dry Soho." (Beattie, ed., 158) She found "lots and lots of artists there"—"established artists" as well as "aspiring" ones. The University of Arizona itself provided much of the impetus for differing views, but the discrete levels of intellectualism in Tucson enriched even the usual university-town milieu, and created what Kingsolver called "a cultural heterogeneity." (Annenberg film)

Kingsolver met people who worked at the Medical School and at the university itself; she met her neighbors and the Mexicans who sold blankets on the street corners, simply because she lived among them. She marveled at the landscapes: being in Arizona "makes you pay attention to color and contrast and hard edges." (qtd. in *Contemporary Authors* 134, 286) She became a part of the community—the farmers' market, the dances, the bar scene—and she looked for people in their twenties and thirties who had the same eager expression on their faces and in their eyes that she had.

Amazed at what she had come upon in Tucson, a more varied city than any she had come to know either in Europe or the States, she tried to ferret out its appeal. (She tried to dismiss the home-sickness she felt for Carlisle and her parents; somehow, Kentucky seemed more remote now that she was back in the States than it had seemed while she was abroad.) (*High Tide*, 6) She decided that Tucson was, ultimately, "a place where north meets south and many people are running for their lives, while many others rest easy with the embarrassment of privilege. Others still are trying to find a place in between, a place of honest living where they can abide themselves and one another without howling in the darkness." (*Small Wonder*, 233) If Kingsolver had thought people in Carlisle ran the gamut from rich to poor, she saw immediately in

Tucson what real wealth meant—and what poverty so deep, and fear so immense, could do to the human soul.

In the midst of the educated, intellectual university crowd, Kingsolver found the underground railroad for refugees from El Salvador, Guatemala, and Chile. The Sanctuary movement was run by a few brave North Americans, many of them in Arizona, who defied federal and state law because they "placed conscience above law. Their risk was to provide safety for Latin American refugees—many hundreds of them—who faced death in their own countries but could not, though innocent of any crime or ill will, gain legal entry into ours." (232) During the late 1970s, Kingsolver became an organizer of the Tucson Committee for Human Rights in Latin America, an affiliate of the national group Committee in Solidarity with the People of El Salvador (CISPES). She held meetings in her home, printed broadsides, and wrote articles that she tried to publish. (Annenberg film) In her later writings about the movement and her involvement in it, she points out that, unfortunately, the dictators of the involved countries "received hearty support from my government." (*Small Wonder*, 232) Additionally, "some of the police who tortured protesters in those countries had been trained in that skill at a camp in Fort Benning, Georgia." When her parents worried about her activities, she tried to place American politics into an historical context:

> Dissidents innocent of any crime greater than a belief in fair treatment of our poorest and ill-treated citizens have died right here on American soil for our freedom, as tragically as any soldier in any war: Karen Silkwood, Medgar Evers, Malcolm X, Denise McNair, Cynthia Wesley, Carole Robertson, Addie Mae Collins, Martin Luther King, Jr., Albert Parsons, August Spies, Adolph Fisher, George Engel, Joe Hill, Nicola Sacco, Bartolomeo Vanzetti.... (*Small Wonder*, 241)

Her parents still worried.

She wrote poems during this period, too. Her friend Rebeca Cartes, who later translated her poems into Spanish, felt that Kingsolver had the empathy in her art to speak for the refugees.

(Annenberg film) "Refuge," in which she uses the metaphor of rape to describe the use made of the unwanted immigrant to the States, is the most dramatic of her works from this period. (*Another America*, 21, 29) The central image—of the quester's hand being severed for his audacity in coming to the United States—is placed in the middle of the poem, which is a brief tapestry of official voices and more humane ones, all speaking English. "In Exile" places a friend, "a ghost-woman," back in Santiago, "[I]nvisible as a decade without days." The poem recalls the Chileans who died or were forced into exile:

> Their colors bled out through the last
> open doors of Chile
> while Victor Jara curled his soul in his fist
> and threw it to a cold star....
>
> (*Another America*, 29)

But it is not only the refugees who have lost their countries; disaffiliation is everywhere. As she writes in "Escape,"

> I have fled my homeland, hopeful
> as a lizard pulling clean from an old skin....
>
> (31)

Kingsolver's words and acts protested the treatment of immigrants in the United States, and she felt she could not support the existing government's policies as long as it continued.

"The other great language of America is Spanish," Kingsolver liked to say, as she tried to learn and practice that other Romance language. (Pence interview, 19) Determined to find roads into the culture that enclosed traditional mainstream Arizona, she put herself in places where Spanish would be the only language spoken. She didn't see her experiences as risky; in fact, she was confident that "[her] adulthood commenced in Tucson, Arizona." (*Small Wonder*, 232) She made a good paycheck; she had regular work that was professional; she had her own private living space and time to keep on writing. She thought often of the advice of one

DePauw professor—"Write sonnets. It will teach you discipline." (231) But she wrote free-form poems, as well, and fiction.

Some of this writing came easily ("like channeling"), but most of it was self-conscious. (Beattie, ed., 157) Turning more ambitious, Kingsolver started to think in terms of longer stories. She recently recalled starting her first novel, which remains unfinished; to her now it seems "hideously uninteresting." (157)

She was happy. She had moved from the apartment to "a little stuccoed house in a neighborhood of barking dogs and front-yard shrines to the Virgin of Guadalupe." (*High Tide*, 18) She was content having land for a vegetable garden, driving near "a Yaqui village that is fringe-edged and small like a postage stamp, and every bit alive." (21) "Pascua Yaqui is a sovereign world," she wrote; "I come here every Easter to watch an irresistible pageant combining deer dances with crucifixion. Like the Tohono O'odham singing down the rain, the masked Yaqui dancers listen for the heartbeat of creation." With her characteristic humor, she points out that near the site of the deer dances is a twelve-screen cinema complex. (Pence interview, 14)

Arizona is not perfect, for all its wealth of people and custom; one must part the curtains of mechanized civilization to unearth the ritual that makes people human. As Kingsolver said in an interview for *Poets & Writers*, "as a species we crave ceremony. All animals have their ceremonies, and ours are very social; we do things in groups.... [W]e secretly crave ceremony and ritual and things that can't be explained.... We need things no one can explain." (21)

In 1979, Kingsolver met the man she would eventually marry. As assistant chemistry professor on the tenure track at University of Arizona, Joe Hoffmann appreciated the person Kingsolver was and was becoming, but he also appreciated all she knew, and felt, about science. He encouraged her to apply for graduate programs in biology and ecology.

Content with her already interesting life, Kingsolver put the applications on hold. She was learning the cultural, natural, and political facets of the state. In love with what she called the "fragile beauties" (Annenberg CPB film) of Arizona, Kingsolver turned to an ecological activism that paralleled her involvement in the Sanctuary movement and in the protests against nuclear sites such as the Palo Verde plant near Phoenix. (Annenberg)

Yet the prospect of being a graduate student began to appeal to her. As a graduate student, she would receive a teaching assistantship, so she would have money to live on, and she would receive help with tuition: she was still hungry to learn. She applied to graduate programs in biology and ecology at Harvard, where E.O. Wilson taught; at Northwestern, for the excellence of its sciences; and to the respected Department of Ecology and Evolutionary Biology at the University of Arizona. With her *magna cum laude* degree from a good liberal-arts college, and letters of recommendation from Dr. Adams and other of her professors there, she was admitted to all three programs. She chose to stay in Arizona, moving into a small, yellow-brick house near campus so she could bike to classes.

She began the doctoral program in 1979. Besides many classes, she was asked to do field research, as well as to teach courses. (Wagner-Martin interview) Her funding was in the form of a teaching assistantship, so for several semesters she taught an introductory course in biology. Then, as she progressed through her own coursework, she was asked to teach an upper-level course for majors in botany, and then another at that level in ecology. Within her first five semesters of study, she had taken all required coursework, studied for and taken her preliminary examinations, and chosen a dissertation topic. (Wagner-Martin)

Kingsolver could see that she could readily complete her degree within another year or year and a half. Her topic, the kin selection systems of eusocial insects, was in the newest area of sociobiology; such an emphasis was heavily mathematical and more theoretical than work in field biology. As she wrote recently, she was "studying a species of termite whose reproductive strategies (sexual vs. asexual) could be predicted with a mathematical model I developed based on the relatedness of individuals within the colony, and how it changed over time.... It was highly theoretical work, relevant to ideas about kin selection that were on the forefront of evolutionary theory work of the time." (Wagner-Martin) She liked the mathematical modeling; she liked the originality of the research area. Her committee members were excited about her work. Kingsolver herself, however, had begun to question the narrowness of doctoral research, a focus she saw as "ultracompetitive" and limiting. (Beattie, ed., 159)

Then, in 1981, a professional job as a science writer opened on the University of Arizona campus in the Office of Arid Lands Studies, a part of the Bioresources Research facility. Asking for a leave of absence from her doctoral program, she took a master's degree and began earning her living through writing. She was writing every day—"sometimes boring days, sometimes kind of fun days, but on Friday I got a check for it." (159) In her capacity as researcher and writer, she published "Euphorbia *Biomass 2*" (1982) and, as second author following Joseph J. Hoffmann as first author, "Products from Desert Plants: A Multi-Process Approach to Biomass Conversion" for the Bioresources Research Facility at the University of Arizona (1983).[1] That same year, with Steven P. McLaughlin as first author, Kingsolver as second, and Hoffmann as third, she published "Biocrude Production in Arid Lands" in *Economic Botany*.

More interesting to Kingsolver than her work as a science writer, which also included numerous freelance opportunities, was her venture into journalism for local newspapers. By 1983, she had reduced her work at the Office of Arid Lands Studies to four days a week; the next year, she went to a three-day position. Eventually, she could support herself through her freelance journalism for several Arizona papers and magazines, as well as national venues.

After leaving her doctoral program, she had audited a fiction-writing workshop given by the well-regarded novelist Francine Prose. As she always did, Kingsolver worked hard, diligently—but until Prose handed her Bobbie Ann Mason's first book, *Shiloh and Other Stories*, she produced the same kinds of plot-dominated stories that already filled her file cabinet. Mason, a Kentuckian, was writing about the part of the world Kingsolver knew best. She stayed up all night to finish the book and said later that the process was "a life-changing moment for me," for

I suddenly understood that what moved me about those stories was not so much the style or the execution: it was the respect that she has for her people—her characters who are her people—and the simple fact that she deemed them worthy of serious literature. My jaw sort of dropped open, and I just walked around for weeks thinking, "I almost threw that away." I have this wonderful thing, this place I come from, this life of mine, that I've been trying to ignore. Not just ignore, that I've been trying to pretend never existed. (Beattie, ed., 157)

Reminiscent of Sherwood Anderson's advice to the young William Faulkner about taking that "little postage-stamp of soil" there in Mississippi as his writing territory, Prose in effect gave Kingsolver back her own country, and she put that direction into practice. The first story Kingsolver wrote that satisfied her aim, to give readers an accessible story that was also true to the place and characters of its being, was "Rose-Johnny," a story she finished and mailed out to *The Virginia Quarterly Review*, where it was accepted with no revision. When she received the $300 check in the mail, she went out and bought as many reams of paper as she could carry; and in her diary, in 1982, in the center of an otherwise blank page, she wrote, "I am a writer." (158) Never confident about her scribbling poems in the margins of notebooks, usually hesitant to admit that she wanted to write professionally, Kingsolver saw her own admission, in writing, as a significant step.

Her fiction increasingly benefited from a quality of style that she learned from Bobbie Ann Mason's work. As she described that aspect, "What moves me most … is that when her characters speak, I hear them exactly. I'm hearing exact inflections, and it makes me homesick. I would say, for me, that's not what I'm trying to do as a writer. What I'm trying to do is … [convey] that burden of truth, of people who have had their voices stolen from them." (157–158) Still intent on what her stories must say, she appreciated the fact that there are several levels of language in a Mason story—the believable language of the characters, which might not necessarily be the language of the story entire.

So Kingsolver tried to find ways of giving the characters in her fiction that immediate diction, while not robbing the story of larger truths. In "Rose-Johnny," the language that becomes so memorable belongs in part to the title character, an unconventional woman whose sexual preferences—and whose family's history of mixed marriage—have made her an outcast. But the heart of the story, the dominant plot, is the skirmish between the story's adult characters and the ten-year-old Georgeann. The adult views are the community's censure of the low-born Rose-Johnny. Georgeann's is the reasonable voice.

In the tale of cruelty based on racial and sexual difference and the small town's abhorrence of that difference, the child narrator secretly becomes the friend of the title character, said to be "Lebanese" (rather than "lesbian") by her schoolteacher aunt. She is neither.

In the saga of the town's vendetta, Kingsolver first gives the reader the false comfort of thinking Georgeann can befriend Rose-Johnny. Georgeann becomes heroic: "I was coming to understand that I would not hear the truth about Rose-Johnny from Aunt Minnie or anyone else. I knew, in a manner that went beyond the meanings of words I could not understand that I would not hear the truth about Rose-Johnny from Aunt Minnie or anyone else.... Rose-Johnny was simply herself, and alone." (Kingsolver, *Homeland*, 218) In the story's denouement, though, the town wins. Mary Etta, the older sister, is nearly raped by town hoodlums because they think *she* is the sister who has become friends with Rose-Johnny. And Rose-Johnny and her grandfather disappear, as does their store.

The story of Southern enmity convinces not entirely because of its narrative, but because of the intersection of specific languages within the conflict. Kingsolver's method here differs from the effects she created in "Homeland," when Great Mam's infrequent language was in keeping with the ritualized tone of native culture. When Great Mam says to her great granddaughter, "If it's important, your heart remembers," the sonority is a piece with the rest of the text. (*Homeland*, 6) Contrastingly, in "Survival Zones," the dialogue between Roberta and her daughter-in-law Aggie as they get

Thanksgiving dinner is much less stylized, but still authentic. The older Roberta says she must cover the azalea bush before the frost:

"I've kept that thing alive for twenty-odd years now. It'd be a shame to see it killed by frost; it's real pretty in the spring. But azalea bushes oughtn't to be growing this far north."

"What do you mean, oughtn't to be?" Aggie, who is paring radish rosebuds now for the relish tray, seems indifferent to the azalea.

"Most of the azaleas aren't hardy. All the nursery catalogues say that white one won't survive north of zone seven. Right around the Mason-Dixon, in other words."

"Well, how'd it get up here, walk?" Aggie laughs.

"Didn't I ever tell you? Ed's mother planted it when they first moved up here. She brought it with her from her people's place in Virginia... She was a good woman, but Lord help me, she was ornery as a tree stump. She's come back and haunt me if I let that azalea die...." (12)

In still other stories, characters use Spanish, "Spanglish," or a kind of lower-class, idiomatic English.

By the time of "Stone Dreams," a story in which the teenaged Julie goes back to Kentucky every summer to spend a few weeks with her grandmother, Kingsolver plays comically with the notion that speech defines character. As the narrator tells her lover, Julie

in the early years would come home with cheerful reports of butter-and-sugar-on-bread for dessert, but more recently she'd brought back a fascination for country speech. 'I'd knock you down for that shirt,' my daughter will cry, and 'Just a minute? I'll just-a-minute you over the head with something!' Last year she filled up a little notebook studying Mother and her rook-playing cronies like Margaret Mead among the Samoans. I was floored to see my mother, policewoman of my adolescence, reduced to a list of quaint phrases. (79)

In the voice of Julie's mother, a married and educated woman going off for a weekend with her lover, the reader "hears" not only speech but a good bit of the story of three generations of women within her family.

Most of the best stories in her story collection *Homeland and Other Stories*, have Kentuckian—or at least Southern—speech, but Kingsolver was trying to write about Arizona. She had learned during her first months living downtown in Tucson that what people saw as "seedy neighborhoods" there constituted a community. The stories she attempted with that setting were interlinked.

She was also writing poetry, partly because poems transferred readily to the broadsides she was distributing about immigration policies, and partly because she had found a distinctive voice in poems that seemed harder to capture in fiction. She describes her first success:

> I entered a poetry contest in, I think, 1981 and, to my absolute astonishment, won, and what that meant is that I had to come down to the university and read this poem and a few others.... [W]hew, boy, that was scary. Not the public speaking aspect of it, but just the public admission that I'd written these personal things and now was going to inflict them upon others. So I did that, and it sort of opened the flood gate. I was invited to other cities. (Beattie, ed., 158)

She also became a part of Tucson's coffee-house culture, taking part in the reading series that were maintained through local talent. Gaining confidence, she sent her work to journals—and poems were accepted.

What had changed that made her poems effective? Kingsolver had learned to transfer the qualities of her mind that made her a scientist; she was learning the role of emotion. Earlier, she had plotted her poems as she did her stories, but then she learned: "I didn't realize that it's *emotion*, not *event*, that creates a dynamic response in the mind of a reader. The artist's job is to sink a taproot in the reader's brain that will grow downward and find a path into the reader's soul and experience, so that some new emotional inflorescence will grow out of it." (*High Tide*, 250)

CHAPTER FIVE

Holding the Line
and *The Bean Trees*

Holding the Line *was a watershed event for me because it taught me to pay attention: to know the place where I lived. Since then I've written other books, most of them set in the vine-scented, dusty climate of Southwestern class struggle....*

—Barbara Kingsolver, introduction
to *Holding the Line*

ONE INTERFACE BETWEEN Kingsolver's immersion in hard science through her years of graduate school and scientific writing, and her creation of characters for her fiction is her experience as journalist covering the 1983–84 Phelps Dodge copper mine strike. Able to hear the stories, inflected with Spanish, both in person and on tape; able to know the people who truly labored for their pay, the well-educated white woman who was so representative of mainstream middle-class culture learned for the first time to *identify*. Being friends with the poor and the hardworking was no longer something the liberal Kingsolver felt morally compelled to do; it was something she *wanted* to do, for she liked—and understood—those strikers and their families. She also greatly admired them.

At first, when she began driving the hundred miles to the strike site, Kingsolver saw her involvement in the strike as a kind of cultural anthropology. She learned about the history of copper mining, the history of Phelps Dodge and its workers—many of them brought in from Mexico to fill the lowest-paying ranks of the company's labor force—and the history of company towns in the Southwest. More specifically, however, she became immersed in the oddities of this particular strike, a strike that soon became the action of women strikers against the mega-corporation. Once the strike began on July 1, 1983, Phelps Dodge adopted such punitive measures against the strikers that most of the male employees of the mines had to leave their towns to seek other kinds of work in other locations: their families could not live on the $40-a-week strike pay. Their wives, then, as members of the Women's Auxiliary—in the company of some of the women employees of the mine—maintained the picket lines. To all appearances, then, the Phelps Dodge strike was one of women against corporation.

Unfortunately for the politics of strike settlement, the Phelps Dodge strike followed the surprising outcome of the PATCO controversy. When, in 1981, then-President Ronald Reagan replaced the striking workers of the Professional Air Traffic Controllers organization, he severely curtailed all union power. When more than 2,300 workers from the thirteen unions connected with the Phelps Dodge mines in four southeastern Arizona locations walked out, rather than negotiate seriously, the company tried to replace them—at first with other employees of the company, and later with outsiders hired as permanent workers. (Aulette and Mills, 252) Because the other Arizona mining companies—with which Phelps Dodge usually stood in a consortium—had already settled union demands, only Phelps Dodge, the largest, created the impasse.

Located in the Arizona towns of Ajo, Bisbee, Douglas, and Morenci (and its sister area, Clifton, separated from Morenci, the mine site, only by the San Francisco River), Phelps Dodge had existed since the 1850s, when it came in from New York state, a white Protestant corporation. Even as managerial control remained with the Anglos, the workers were "Cornish ('Cousin Jacks'), Welsh, German, Swedish, Spanish and Italian craftsmen, with workers from China, Mexico, the adjacent American states as well as the Navajo reservations. The Mexican workers, who made up as much as 80 percent of all laborers (exclusive of craftsmen), were considered by many the best smelter workers." (Rosenblum, 19) Because of the racial mix, and the predominance of Mexican labor, only the Wobblies (the Industrial Workers of the World, or IWW) attempted to start unions there. Truly paternalistic, Phelps Dodge created towns, with management housed on the upper mountainsides, laborers in areas more likely to flood, and, in another area, Native Americans in shacks and tents rather than houses. (Kingsolver, *Holding the Line*, 65) In Morenci, the company owned the stores and services as well as the real estate; sometimes, workers were paid in company scrip. Assessing the kind of control the company maintained, Kingsolver concluded, "A Phelps Dodge town ... is a frontier phenomenon." (65)

In 1983, however, times were less prosperous for the copper industry (stymied by the 1982 recession and the curtailment of auto production), so all unions were calling for freezes in pay. The Phelps Dodge employees agreed to that part of the contract, but they wanted their cost-of-living adjustments and medical benefits continued. And they did not want the "26 and 2" work schedule (26 days on followed by 2 days off) reactivated. (Rosenblum, 71) There were other less-than-humane provisions in the contract drafts, as well. Even though mine employees and their union representatives could see that Phelps Dodge was trying to provoke a strike, they were confident in the power of their cohesive strength: they had lived through strikes before—once for several years—and they believed in the unions. Their fathers and grandfathers had been Phelps Dodge employees; it was a family tradition—to work, to strike, and to work again.

The day the strike began, however, the company trucked in 1,400 supplemental workers; for the first time in mining history, the mines were not shut down for a strike. In that one change of operation, the unions lost irrevocable power. Once the picket lines were up and staffed, even though the replacement workers had no qualms about crossing them (and sometimes threw pennies at the striking workers and their children), Phelps Dodge employees, buttressed by mainstream media, talked about the violence, the anger, of the strikers. In a few weeks Governor Bruce Babbitt sent in "over 400 state troopers and 300 National Guard" to "control" the strikers. (Aulette and Mills, 254) Kingsolver described the conflict:

> Within a month, events had turned in a way I'd never seen before, nor heard of happening in my lifetime.... People were being jailed for infractions no larger than picking up the phone and calling a neighbor 'scab.' Helicopters and squads of armored men with tear gas and large automatic weapons were storming tiny, bucolic Main Streets, and strike supporters were claiming their right to hold the line with extraordinary resistance. The faces and hands of this resistance mostly belonged to women. (*Holding*, xiii)

For historians Rosenblum, Aulette and Mills, the strike and the Phelps Dodge part in it—supported by a cadre of labor and economics scholars from the Wharton School of Business at the University of Pennsylvania—represented the repression of workers based on both ethnicity and gender. Aulette and Mills point out that whereas the Mexican workers were the backbone of the union, the "scabs," the replacement workers, were white; they conclude "the company used ethnicity ... to divide the strikers." (Aulette and Mills, 254) They also noted that the enforcement troops "treated the Hispanic strikers more harshly." This ethnic blanket was also a means of attacking the women, because many of the women on the picket lines were also of Hispanic origin. For Kingsolver, however, the individual stories of the hundreds of people caught in the dilemma—betrayed by the company for which their families had worked for generations, forced to live in poverty while they tried to find justice in their workplace, and finally wronged by most of the representations of their identities and their struggle—were the core of the event.

When she first went to the site of the greatest controversy, the Morenci mine, few journalists had been around—at least, this tall woman in jeans, driving an old Nissan pickup truck, seemed to attract unusual attention. Hostile to manufacturing that was being taken out of the United States, the miners challenged her truck, a Japanese product. She calmed them down by telling them it was put together in the States—whether or not that was accurate. From those early days of the freelance journalist's asking questions and generally snooping around, they accepted Kingsolver's presence, in part for its frequency, and in part because of a rumor that she was writing a book. It was only a few weeks into her coverage of the strike that Kingsolver learned a valuable lesson: impartiality was impossible. The notion of "objective" journalism was a fallacy.

Long fascinated by the power of strong women in all areas of life, Kingsolver found it easier to talk with the women on the picket line than with the men. She also was in a kind of revolt from what she saw as the sterile, ivory-tower specialization of academic life: surrounded all her years of graduate school by people who had one slim focus in their professional work, she had left her doctoral program in order to find a broader application of knowledge. Working now as a scientific writer, she knew that her strengths in that work were precision and clarity. She knew she could excel in that kind of writing. But she still wanted a deeper immersion in life—the tangible world in which she could see her vegetables growing—and, although her shyness kept her from making numerous contacts, she also felt a keen empathy with people. To interview the Phelps Dodge strikers, to become a part of their embattled community, appealed to many facets of Kingsolver's emerging and maturing self.

Several years after the eighteen months of the strike proper, when Kingsolver began to write the book which would become *Holding the Line*, she had already mythologized the women of the Morenci picket line. She imagistically connected them with Maxine Hong Kingston's creation of the Chinese "woman warrior," the girl grown to womanhood with the gift of leadership, the woman who sees life as sacrificial—but also as courageous. Kingston's woman warrior is no martyr. Neither are Kingsolver's women on the strike lines. As she wrote, after a specific reference to Emile Zola's novel *Germinal*, about women laborers and protests: "This is the fortune of the woman warrior, too frail to defend her nation in battle but sturdy enough to take her nation's gunfire in a strike. Every tradition has its price, and most have been bought and sold many times over—history often decides that a woman's place is to do the work of men for half the pay." (*Holding*, 10)

The very organization of *Holding the Line* is character-based. Unlike most of Kingsolver's later novels, which are driven by theme, by the ideas she wants to be sure to express, this work which might well have been handled chronologically, as the history of this act followed by that one, plays out as women's stories. The first chapter, for example, begins with the narrative of Flossie Navarro, a woman mine employee close to seventy years old at the time the strike begins, who chose to work in the Morenci mine because it was closest to her beloved Arkansas. Kingsolver moves from the Navarro story—to which she returns elsewhere in the book—to the narratives of Jamie Ramon, employed since 1973 at the Ajo mine; the slight Betty Copeland, who literally weighs 92 pounds; and Jean Lopez, from the Bisbee mine, whose modest reply to the interviewing journalist was that she was "Nobody really, just a mom." (4)

The first chapter of the book, "The Devil's Domain," sets the stories about women into the masculinist context: mining is a man's occupation. Women, in fact, are said to jinx the work—they are representatives of the Devil. Kingsolver's whole discussion of gendered roles, and the surprise of finding that the picketers were largely women, stems from the mine industry's belief that women "have no business with a mine." In the second chapter, "On the Line," Kingsolver presents a brisk history of unions in the industry, as well as of mining itself, particularly the racism evident in the rates of pay, living accommodations, treatment, and the kinds of work given to non-white workers. She here discusses the terms of the proposed 1983 contract, and she emphasizes the shock of the Arizona strikers when the National Guard arrived with its tanks, trucks, SWAT teams, and snipers.

Chapter Three, "Hell and High Water," describes vividly the destruction of the San Francisco River flood during the late summer. One third of the area's 1,800 houses vanished—either in the flood itself or in the masses of mud that obliterated possessions and entire structures. As she charts individual stories of great damage, one of the emphases becomes the quotation she chooses as the title for Chapter Four, "We'll Stay Here Until We're Gone," a line spoken by the indomitable Flossie Navarro. Increasingly woven into the poignant stories of the strikers is Kingsolver's belief that the National Guard, the forces that were earlier brought in only to quell the strike, did very little to help during the time of natural disaster. People were left to starve, languish, live in caves or shelters maintained by the Red Cross—as if nature were conspiring with the Phelps Dodge management, which continued to operate the mines by escorting or trucking in the replacement workers. Or, as Carmina Garcia reminded Kingsolver when she asked whether or not the displaced people had thought of leaving Morenci or Clifton, "Leave? Where else can you go?" (65)

As the remainder of *Holding the Line* rolls out one horrifying episode after another, the reader recalls Kingsolver's observation that the individual tapes of people's stories that she recorded—hundreds of them—compose a kind of "community journal spoken aloud." (Annenberg film) Long after she left Clifton, she realized that in those "hundreds and hundreds of hours" of listening to the voices, speaking in their effective mixture of Spanish and English, she had "learned the language of Arizona." (Annenberg)

The first national publication of any of this material for Kingsolver appeared in the magazine *The Progressive*, co-authored with Jill Barrett Fein, who was herself a union member of the Railway and Airline Clerks. With a photo of the Arizona women on the picket line, the short article described the arrival of the National Guard using the words of "miner" Jamie Ramon: "Suddenly, six cars pulled up and state troopers jumped out with machine guns. Not one of us had any weapon other than a baseball bat." (Fein interview, 15) The story focused on the needs of the strikers, once they had returned from jail to find that Phelps Dodge had shut off their electricity, foreclosed on mortgages, and evicted them. Excited by the tangible proof that her words could effect understanding, Kingsolver wrote portions of the story with more of a eye to publishing a book. At that time she read through the agents section of a writer's directory and came across the advertisement for the woman who became her very effective agent, Frances Goldin. Clearly, Kingsolver was thinking of herself as a writer—a role she had not yet wholeheartedly assumed.

In the last chapters of *Holding the Line*, she surveyed the next year of events, always focusing the reader's attention on the endurance of the wives and families who subsisted in terrible conditions, in order to further their families' traditions of fair pay and benefits for good work. She discusses the ongoing brutality, the cavalier treatment of particularly the women, and the anniversary-marking violence of July 1, 1984. But throughout she keeps the reader's attention on the stories of the strikers, sometimes through using their words as chapter titles ("We Go with Our Heads Up," "My Union and My Friends," "Just a Bunch of Ladies") but frequently by letting the narrative of one person center the chapter. The reader finds that a chapter which covers more specific history still opens with a story about a person who is either amazingly resilient or unbelievably foolhardy—but always for the cause of the community and the group, rather than for individual self-aggrandizement.

Although *Holding the Line* has its moments of triumph, and the women who have become characters are themselves memorable in Kingsolver's treatment, the story is bleak. As historian Jonathan Rosenblum wrote succinctly, the story of the Phelps Dodge strike and its unfavorable resolution is the story of "why some 2,000 Arizona copper workers sacrificed so much only to see livelihoods, friendships, and even communities dissolve." (Rosenblum, 8) Further, Phelps Dodge's anti-union stand destroyed "the entire bargaining structure in the copper industry." (10)

In her coverage of the strike, and in her careful accumulation of the tapes she stored in shoeboxes, Kingsolver had come to a new understanding of the power the story of injustice could have if it were properly presented. She was beginning to see how important a writer's work could become in the whole scheme of human life.

Still working for the Office of Arid Lands and now married to her busy scholar husband, Kingsolver was still active in the Sanctuary movement and still writing fiction and sharing it with friends. When she showed Janice Bowers a story she called "The

One to Get Away," once again set in Kentucky, she was surprised at her writer friend's comment that this was not just a story. (Beattie, ed., 160) Rather, Bowers thought, it was the beginning of a novel.

Months passed. Kingsolver toyed with idea that the young woman character who was running away from the stultifying small Kentucky town could become a full-fledged protagonist. She seemed to have less and less time for serious writing. But then, pregnant with her first child, Kingsolver was beset with one of the problems of pregnancy—insomnia. Exhausted from her inability to sleep, she consulted a doctor who told her to do something unpleasant during that wakeful time, rather than rewarding herself. He suggested scrubbing the grout on the bathroom tile. Instead, Kingsolver got out the story that might become a novel.

She knew four things when she began the project, writing in a closet so that the light would not awaken her spouse. The first was that she liked the voice of the young Kentucky woman character. Whether or not it would hold up through a book-length narrative, only the writing would decide. On page two of the story, for instance, her character reflected,

> Missy was what everyone called me, not that it was my name, but because when I was three supposedly I stamped my foot and told my own mother not to call me Marietta but *Miss* Marietta, as I had to call all the people including children in the houses where she worked Miss this or Mister that, and so she did from that day forward. Miss Marietta and later on just Missy. (Kingsolver, *The Bean Trees*, 2)

Too, Kingsolver liked the concept that this part of Tucson, which she had been trying to write about earlier, would finally be fictionalized. She had needed a way to bring characters like Lou Ann Ruiz into a different mix, and using Taylor Greer's voice might do the trick: "What I needed was an outsider's take on this place that most people would consider a bad piece of real estate, but really it's this rich, lively, symbiotic, interconnected community of women." It will be the narrator, Taylor, "who gets in the car in Kentucky and drives across the country and slams into it by accident," who "will really see." (Beattie, ed., 160)

Third, she knew that a novel—particularly a first novel—had to be something like a purse, "a thing that somebody's been wanting to write all their lives":

> I think of it as your whole life long you've been carrying this big old purse, and every time you come upon something, a pretty rock or something, you put it in there. Then comes the day where it's too heavy, you can't carry it around anymore, and you sit down at a table and you just dump everything out. And kaboom! there it all is. (160)

The fourth of Kingsolver's realizations had to do with her (and her father's) eternal optimism, this trait in conjunction with what she had learned through many years of reading the fiction of Flannery O'Connor. She had recognized that humor could leaven the heaviest of substances. The story of the abused Indian child, Turtle, left in the care of an unemployed and largely uneducated young stranger, appeared to be anything but comic. But in Kingsolver's treatment, that story became bearable. As she said in the *Poets & Writers* interview, "the biggest thing I learned from Flannery O'Connor is that life's blackest truths have to be told with a punch line. I don't think it's dishonest or inappropriate.... Life is just awful and hysterically funny." (Pence interview, 21)

Taking as her mantra as a fiction writer "[j]ust to see people survive ... to live through mean times without becoming mean-spirited," (Epstein interview, *The Progressive*, 34) Kingsolver devised a succession of early chapters that both introduced the central characters and then set the elements of plot in place. These discrete sections of *The Bean Trees* are themselves fascinating. The first chapter sets Taylor on her way, and has her receiving the abused Native American child in the dark parking lot. "New Year's Pig" presents the young mother Lou Ann Ruiz, facing divorce, her infant son, unemployability, and basement-level self esteem, yet ready to help Taylor with her newly acquired three-year-old. "Jesus Is Lord Used Tires" presents the wryly humane Mattie, a source of

Providence at every turn. Assembling her cast of women characters, Kingsolver also moves the narrative along so that by the sixth chapter, not quite a third of the way through the novel, Taylor Greer has a place to live, a job, and childcare for the clinging (and not yet talking) Turtle. She has found her soulmate in the Kentucky-born Lou Ann Ruiz. The only problematic characters are the neighbor "ladies," Virgie Mae Parsons and Edna Poppy, who make racist and critical comments about everyone. They too will have unusual stories.

In Kingsolver's admission, "I think our first responsibility, and also our first treasure as writers, is to represent ourselves. So women are always dead center in my novels. And my novels are about the things women think most about, like keeping our children fed, and how to manage on not very much income." (Epstein interview, 34) Mattie is the resolution of most of the roles women must play; it is she who works for the Guatemalan refugees through the Sanctuary movement. When Taylor and Lou Ann meet Estevan and his wife, Esperanza, fleeing from their country, the group of close friends—with Mattie at their center—is complete.

They live throughout the "seedy" neighborhood—Mattie at Jesus Is Lord Used Tires, Taylor and Turtle at the Republic Hotel—until they become housemates of Lou Ann and Dwayne Ray. In the racist climate of lower-class Tucson, ironically, the darker-skinned Turtle, Lou Ann's infant son, and the Guatemalan refugees thrive. Finally, trusting to the love that has come to surround her, the silent Turtle speaks. Her first word is "Bean"—and its variation, "Humbean."

With her vocabulary increasing vegetable by vegetable (because the growth of a plant is one of the few predictable elements in life), Turtle shows that she is smart, funny, and loving. She finally christens the wisteria, past its bloom and filled with pods, by calling it a "bean tree." Taylor's plan to adopt the child runs parallel with the Sanctuary movement's need to get Estevan and the depressed Esperanza to Oklahoma, where they will be safer.

After Esperanza's suicide attempt, Estevan and Taylor spend an evening together. As Estevan tells Taylor about the persecution they faced in Guatemala, and the fact that their relatives were murdered and their daughter, Ismene, taken, remote political history becomes personal. Because the two of them knew the names of seventeen Sanctuary cell members, their child became the pawn: only if they told the authorities the seventeen names would their daughter be returned to them. They did not tell. They *could* not tell. As a result of Estevan's telling Taylor their story, and the intimacy the story created, Taylor feels sympathy for Esperanza: "All of Esperanza's hurts flamed up in my mind, a huge pile of burning things that the world just kept throwing more onto. Somewhere in that pile was a child that looked just like Turtle."

In her narrative alternation between the tragic and the humorous, Kingsolver begins the move to climactic, significant action. Just when the reader thinks the most important plotline is Lou Ann's finding a job, the political atmosphere darkens. An exchange between Mattie and Taylor reveals Taylor's naivety:

> "Immigration is making noises. They could come in and arrest [Estevan and Esperanza], and they'd be deported before you even had time to sit down and think about it."
> "Here?" I asked. "They would come into your house?"

No one is safe from either deportation or persecution. Mattie repeats, "The only legal way a person from Guatemala can stay here is if they can prove in court that their life was in danger when they left.... When people run for their lives they frequently neglect to bring along their file cabinets of evidence." (*High Tide*, 140)

The novel ends with the road trip to Oklahoma—Taylor driving Mattie's Lincoln with Esperanza, Estevan, and Turtle as passengers. On the long trip, Turtle "told Esperanza a kind of ongoing story, which lasted for hundreds of miles and sounded like a vegetarian's version of Aesop's Fables." Taylor adopts Turtle (illegally) and leaves the refugees in a safe house. Then she and Turtle head home. *The Bean Trees* is, finally, a novel mostly about the varieties of "home," and the many varieties of "families."

Both are concepts Kingsolver has questioned. The traditional definitions of each—the house with the picket fence on its own half-acre of land, and, living inside it, a father, a mother, and 2.4 children—are images that leave out more people than they encompass. As she wrote in her essay "Stone Soup":

> Families change, and remain the same. Why are our names for home so slow to catch up to the truth of where we live? ... [I]t's probably been suggested to you in a hundred ways that yours isn't exactly a real family, but an imposter family, a harbinger of cultural ruin, a slapdash substitute.... (*High Tide*, 136)

One of the themes of *The Bean Trees* is that there are dangers in ostracizing people who form nontraditional families from those around them—the single parent like Taylor, the divorced parent like Lou Ann, the childless couples like Estevan and Esperanza or Mrs. Parsons and Edna Poppy, or especially Mattie, who has "something like" grandchildren, the children of the refugees she helps through Sanctuary. Each adult Kingsolver writes about in this novel belongs to a non-traditional family. With surprisingly little didacticism, the novel expresses the author's belief that "[d]ivorce, remarriage, single parenthood, gay parents, and blended families simply are." (136)

The Bean Trees also shows its author's love of nature. Not only does the gardening—the sheer love of plants and flowers that both Mattie and Taylor evince—bring Turtle to her very personal speech, but the natural world gives Taylor and Turtle their moment of fond resolution in Oklahoma, before they start the long trip home. In the book's last chapter, titled "Rhizobia," Kingsolver places Taylor with Turtle in the Oklahoma City Main Library. As they look through the *Horticultural Encyclopedia*, which "had pictures of vegetables and flowers that were far beyond both her vocabulary and mine," the child points out the wisteria: "Turtle was thrilled. She slapped the picture enthusiastically, causing the young man at the reference desk to look over his glasses at us. The book had to have been worth a hundred dollars at least, and it was very clean." As Taylor whispers the wisteria's story to Turtle, she comes to the word *rhizobia*—microbes that live on plant's roots and re-oxygenate it even in the poorest of soils.

The plant lives largely because of its separate support system. Or, in Taylor's words, "The wisteria vines on their own would just barely get by ... but put them together with rhizobia and they make miracles." The reader is led to imagine yet another kind of family.

When Kingsolver finished the book, not even sure it was a novel, she sent it to the agent who had assumed that, where Kingsolver was concerned, she would be sending the nonfiction book about the Phelps Dodge Copper strike. Luckily, Frances Goldin recognized the strengths of *The Bean Trees;* she sent it to several publishers. The offer from Houghton Mifflin was low, so she rejected it. When Kingsolver protested her declining that offer, Goldin told her to value her own work and to understand how publishing works: "If they pay you a moderately large advance, then they will put a moderately large amount of effort into promoting the book and insuring they get that advance back. You, the writer, are not the issue. The issue is their investment." (Beattie, ed., 162)

The next offer was from HarperCollins, and the advance was enough for Kingsolver to live on for a year. Goldin accepted the deal and Kingsolver signed the contract on the day she returned from the hospital after the birth of her daughter, Camille. Thinking of herself as both a mother and a novelist simultaneously was difficult. It was to set Kingsolver's agenda for the rest of her life.

CHAPTER SIX

A Mother
and a Novelist

[I]t [The Bean Trees] *tells "the story of ordinary
people who understand both realities [of invasion]
as they touch their own ... a story about racism,
sexism and dignity."*
    —Margaret Randall, *The Women's Review of Books*

IT WAS A TIME of excitement, happiness, and the inevitable
exhaustion. Would the baby be able to exist on her mother's breast
milk? Would she begin sleeping through the night? Would the fact
that the family lived two thousand miles away from the Kingsolver
grandparents and aunts and uncles be difficult for not only the
mother but eventually for the child? Questions about those vexing
words—*home* and *family*—underlay Kingsolver's anxieties about
following through professionally as a writer.

She began a schedule that would allow her to stay with her
writing. As she described daily life in the Arizona household,
besides the time spent watching and marveling at the baby, she
and her husband worked out a division of time that, of course,
privileged what the baby needed but also privileged Kingsolver's
hours as writer. She recalled, "I would start at four or five in the
morning and write until noon, and he would take care of Camille

in the morning and then he'd go into work [at the University of Arizona] and work late. He'd work noon until nightfall or whatever, and we'd switch.... I nursed her until she was about eight months." (Beattie, ed., 163) At that time, they hired Ethel Briggs, who came to help out a few hours, several days a week.

At the advice of her agent, Kingsolver—in addition to starting serious writing on the Phelps Dodge book—began work on what would become a collection of short stories, very few of which had been published, and many of which were not finished. With the publication of *The Bean Trees* scheduled for the winter, she needed to complete the production responsibilities—going over the copyedited manuscript, carefully reading proofs, helping to compile the review list, and doing as much of the publicity as her publisher asked: how many author biographies would one book necessitate?

The most important element of Kingsolver's accepting the fact that she now had two new roles in life was asking her mother to visit. To meet and help care for the baby was Mrs. Kingsolver's primary reason for coming to Arizona, but Barbara also wanted her to read the typescript of *The Bean Trees*, which she describes in a section of memoir as "the longest letter to you [her mother] I've ever written. Finally, after a thousand tries, I've explained everything I believe in, exactly the way I always wanted to: human rights, Central American refugees, the Problem That Has No Name, abuse of the powerless, racism, poetry, freedom, childhood, motherhood, Sisterhood Is Powerful. All that...." (*Small Wonder*, 170) As her mother read the typescript out on the front-porch glider, Kingsolver waited for her approval—which she did receive.

Beginning new books before the responses to *The Bean Trees* started to arrive was difficult; Kingsolver chose to write things other than a second novel, though she was thinking already about the story that would become the second novel, *Animal Dreams*. She felt competent to write up the strike material in a more academic form: *Holding the Line* could be sociology, though her plan to incorporate a number of taped voices and stories would enliven that kind of work. To some extent, she felt competent to work on short stories, since she had been writing, and trying to write, in that form since undergraduate school. Pulling the short fiction into a whole collection, however, might pose a new kind of problem.

Homeland and Other Stories opened with the title story, the one that Kingsolver thought was the most "spiritually autobiographical" of all her work. The narrative of the Cherokee great-grandmother had been rewritten countless times, but had never been published. Near the end of the collection she placed "Rose-Johnny," the *Virginia Quarterly Review* story which had since been collected in *New Stories from the South* and would soon be adapted as a stage piece. The collection closed with "Why I Am a Danger to the Public," the story she had crafted (with fictional characters) from some of the Phelps Dodge tapes. The long story is told in the fictive voice of Vicki Morales, a native of the copper-mining town of Bolton, New Mexico, and an employee of the Ellington mine. The mother of two children, living without her husband or child support, Vicki is currently on strike. Even more currently, she is in jail, being held for an impossible bond of $500,000. Even in the story's opening, the narrator's voice acknowledges both the mixed-race culture and Vicki's toughness:

> *Bueno,* if I get backed into a corner I can just about raise up the dead. I'll fight, sure. But I'm no lady wrestler. If you could see me you would know this thing is a joke—Tony, my oldest, is already taller than me, and he's only eleven. So why are they so scared of me I have to be in jail? I'll tell you. (*Homeland,* 226)

Vicki rehearses the conditions which led to the strike—"There has never been one that turned so many old friends *chingandose,* not here in Bolton"—and creates characters who are the core union members. This long story, published earlier in *New Times* and revised for the book, is interesting for a quantity of accurate information. Although Kingsolver worked hard to follow those rules from Francine Prose's writing class, the match between point of view (which is Vicky's voice) and subject matter is not quite satisfying.

This story, like others in *Homeland,* shows Kingsolver working to create opening sentences that both grab the reader's attention and lead the reader to a conclusion that fulfills all the promise of the opening. In Prose's directions, "The first sentence of a story or the first paragraph of a novel should make a promise that the rest of the book will keep." (Beattie, ed., 166) One of the previously unpublished stories, "Covered Bridges," opens with such a sentence:

> Last summer all of our friends were divorcing or having babies, as if these were the only two choices. It's silly, I know but it started us thinking. From there our thoughts ran along a track that seemed to stop at every depot and have absolutely no final destination. (*Homeland*, 42)

Told in the voice of the science-teacher husband, it leads to an ending in which the couple decides to have no children, but to remain happily stable within each other's love. In the similarly unpublished "Islands on the Moon," the narrator is Annamarie, a pregnant woman less than pleased with the fact that her aging mother is also pregnant. Here, the older woman's unusual personality is introduced from the start: "Annamarie's mother, Magda, is one of a kind." A more comical story with the perplexing title "Bereaved Apartments" operates the same way. It opens, "*That woman in the gable-ended house is not all there.* In the beginning there is nothing else for Sulie to think...." The technique works well in several of the stronger stories ("Survival Zones," "Jump-Up Day," "Stone Dreams"), but in these, each one of which seems overly long, these openings are probably not comprehensive enough to suggest the range of ideas Kingsolver includes in each story.

After the colloquial fluidity of Kingsolver's writing in *The Bean Trees*, much of the novel's effect tied to the perky narration in Taylor Greer's voice, many of the stories in *Homeland* seem labored. In some of them, the reader is reminded that Kingsolver *is* a novice. How could she be other than that? Yet in compiling stories for this collection, she set herself the task of experimenting with point of view; she said that she did not want to stay the voice of Taylor Greer. She recalled about her *Bean Trees* narrator that she had wanted to tell that story "with a Kentucky accent," in part to make palatable all those weighty themes—"[c]ommunity, responsibility, raising children without violence, the confines of poverty" and, perhaps most important, "the shape of justice." Once that book appeared, however, she wanted people to see that she was a versatile writer. (Annenberg film)

A good story such as "Extinctions" shows Kingsolver aiming high. "It may already be too late for the pandas, the man on TV says." Kingsolver's opening, coupled with the title, takes the reader into the mundane—but humane—lives of Grace, Randall, and their two sons, one of whom reveres dinosaurs and the other, all endangered species. Scolded for her excessive concern about the boys, Grace is a congenital worrier—the worlds of popular culture and television leave her few peaceful moments.

But from the frame of the story, as Grace drives with the boys back to her family's homeplace for Easter dinner and church, the mood of the fiction darkens. In the stories of the family's history runs the current of silently abused children—one of them Grace, the other Nestor Beltrain, the new minister of the Woods Baptist Church. In the jokes the men of Grace's family make, and the excuses the women make, Grace sees clearly that none of them has ever considered what the cruel violence of Nestor's father has created. The irony that the severely damaged Nester is now in charge of people's souls—and that her family goes to that church instead of their own for the "show" of Nestor as minister—disturbs Grace with an intensity she finds hard to fathom. She takes her sons and leaves the family weekend; she does not stay for church. Her act suggests that it is her family that has become the danger to her boys.

"Quality Time," the shortest story in *Homeland*, is one of Kingsolver's best. Appearing first in *Redbook,* the story stays with the Kentucky voice, this time expressing the frantic thoughts of Miriam, a young mother with too little time to do her errands, work, and manage her daughter, Rennie. Breaking with the cultural assumption (the good parent is one who spends "quality time" with the child, regardless of how much actual time he or she has), Kingsolver shows the impossibility of stretching one person's energy and ability over the myriad tasks that occupy Miriam's life. Believing that "organization is the religion of the single parent," she seldom makes exceptions in her schedule. Five-year-old Rennie is her entire life; the story shows that clearly. Driving home from Rennie's daycare, they think of what to have for dinner. One of the most significant paragraphs in the piece is that in which they decide on their menu:

> In the overtones of her voice and the way she pushes her blond hair over her shoulder there is a startling maturity, and Miriam is frozen for a moment with a vision of a much older Rennie. All the different Rennies—the teenager, the adult—are already contained in her hands and her voice, her confidence. From moments like these, parents can find the courage to believe in the resilience of their children's lives. They will barrel forward like engines, armored by their own momentum, more indestructible than love. (*Homeland*, 76)

The dedication of *Homeland and Other Stories* reads "for my family." Kingsolver leaves imprecise whether she is thinking of her immediate family of three, her extended family in Kentucky, or the wider group of people involved intimately with her life. The manuscript was ready to be put into production as soon as *The Bean Trees* was published; it would carry a 1989 publication date. The strategy is that readers who found the novel would soon have another book of her fiction to read, and Kingsolver's reputation would build and grow.

Holding the Line was also nearing completion, but its publication would be of a more academic sort. The general public would probably never know that the Barbara Kingsolver of *The Bean Trees* was also the Barbara Kingsolver of *Holding the Line*, a book slated to appear from ILR Press, sponsored by the New York State School of Industrial and Labor Relations and a subsidiary of Cornell University Press in Ithaca, New York. Because university presses publicize their forthcoming books many months in advance—since their chief avenue of publicity is the firm's catalogue, rather than ads in newspapers or journals—the ILR Press was hopeful that this book would also have a 1989 publication date. In its finishing stages, Kingsolver dedicated the manuscript once again to families: "For the families who held the line, and those who will have to do it again." (*Holding the Line*)

The publication history of Kingsolver's books supports her statement that all her work has been written out of the passions she felt when she was twenty: despite the variety of her forms, her writing is unified thematically. (Epstein interview, 36) That she remained most interested in the stories of women—live women, fictional ones, silenced ones—is remarked in a section of the acknowledgements for *Holding the Line*, when she notes,

> Most of all, I'm indebted to the women of Clifton, Morenci, Ajo, and Douglas, Arizona—whose names essentially comprise the index of this book—who welcomed me into their houses and their lives. Their compassion, resourcefulness, and courage will be an inspiration to me for life. (*Holding the Line*, ix)

More significant to Kingsolver than a historical account of that eighteen-month strike, *Holding the Line* attempted to create for readers "two different kinds of truth," both "human and historical." "Many of the stories are personal, describing an internal landscape," she writes. "Sometimes the most important events were not 'And then they threw me in jail,' but rather, 'For the first time I realized that if newspapers are lying about us, they could be lying about places in the Middle East and Nicaragua.'" (xxi)

Sorting out the mass of detail—the hundreds of lives touched by the 500-some days of strike activity, the hundreds of happenings on the line—was difficult. The freelance Kingsolver could not be on the line every day or every night; when she was absent, she was as likely to be told lies as was any other reporter. As she admitted, "Collecting rumors and trying to assemble truth, I sometimes felt like the foolish heroine of the Rumpelstiltskin story whose brash confidence got her into the job of trying to spin straw into gold." Kingsolver also said that she became "obsessed with verification because, as the strike wore on, the truth was shocking enough without embroidery." (xvi–xxii)

By being on site frequently, however, Kingsolver had more of a sense of what was plausible than many reporters did. She noted with disappointment that sometimes the least accurate account was the "'official' version in the state newspapers." (xxii) To find her way through the mass of material, complete with its mazes of detail, Kingsolver explained, "I applied my training as a scientist, looking for replication of sequence and detail among the stories." (xxii)

Because of the layers of sometimes contradictory detail, the hours of fact-checking, and the hundreds of hours of taped interviews, *Holding the Line* is more than an assembly of facts. It is, in some respects, an account formed by the swell of passion as it unsettled the writer's demeanor of reportorial objectivity. Kingsolver admits to that characteristic, too:

> In a place a few hours drive from where I live, the government, the police, and a mining company formed a conspicuous partnership to break the lives of people standing together for what they thought was right. That ironclad, steel-toed partnership arrested hundreds of citizens on charges so ludicrous that the state, after having perfectly executed its plan of intimidating the leadership and turning public sympathy against the strikers, quietly dropped every case. (xxii)

She had worked too hard not to finish the book, and she had been too disappointed with the authority of the government. She was not going to forget about her years of work in the small mining towns to bask in the success of her novel. So in the flush of her incipient success, Kingsolver wrote *Holding the Line*.

Once the *Publishers Weekly* advance review of *The Bean Trees* appeared on January 15, 1988, Kingsolver allowed herself to believe the praise her agent and her editor at HarperCollins, Janet Goldstein, had been giving her. (Annenberg film) People were calling the firm for advance copies of the book; editors from other publishing houses wanted to know who this Barbara Kingsolver was. The *Publishers Weekly* review could hardly have been better. Called "funny" and "inspiring," *The Bean Trees* was said to be "a marvelous affirmation of risk-taking, commitment and everyday miracles ... an overwhelming delight, as random and unexpected as real life." (Jan. 15, 1988) As the reviewer for *The New York Times Book Review* was to suggest, Kingsolver's book was "the Southern novel taken west" (Butler, 15)—and thereby privy to the same kind of enthusiastic response as Lee Smith's fiction (most recently, her *Fair and Tender Ladies*) or the first novel by Kaye Gibbons, another Southern writer, whose *Ellen Foster* was a runaway success. The combination of realism and humor appealed to readers who had come to identify women's writing with sharp, and usually relentless, pain.

In *The New York Times Book Review*, Jack Butler commented on the book's vivid language, which worked like a poem, despite the sense of realism. Hyperbolic in its praise, the review appeared on April 10, 1988. It followed brief praise in *The New Yorker* (April 4, 1988, 101–102) and some excellent March reviews in newspapers, among them Patricia Holt's rave comments in *The San Francisco Chronicle*: "So wry and wise we wish it would never end." (Holt, 1) She especially liked the "chatty, down-home audacity" of its language.

While both *The Christian Science Monitor* and *Ms.* were pleased with the book during that heady month of April, the *Ms.* reviewer, Karen Fitzgerald, mentioned that for some readers *The Bean Trees* might be a bit too politically correct, though she admired Kingsolver's characters and language. (Fitzgerald, 28) It took Margaret Randall's thoughtful review in *The Women's Review of Books*, beginning on page 1 of the May issue, to help place *The Bean Trees* as something other than a glib voicing of the comic Southern women's novel. Randall, herself one of the more politically active of the literati, saw the book's strengths as its voice, language, and sense of community, but she also insisted that it was a very serious book, in which "the sexual invasion of the child's body and the political invasion of a nation's sovereignty" run parallel. (Randall, 1, 3)

So far as the writing is concerned, Randall says that Kingsolver has "a marvelous ear, a fast-moving humor and the powerful undercurrent of human struggle." In places the book is "hilariously funny." And structurally, it keeps the reader involved: "There are surprises in the book. There is adventure. And there is resolution, as believable as it is gratifying." So far as Kingsolver's personal history, Randall's title for the review, "Human Comedy," was an echo of William Saroyan's *The Human Comedy,* the novel that had been so important to her in Carlisle, Kentucky.

It wasn't only the early reviews that were overwhelmingly positive; the book's reception grew with each review, and Kingsolver was grateful that the publicity department at HarperCollins sent her groups of reviews every few weeks. Good news came as well from librarians and booksellers, news beyond sales figures—*The Bean Trees* had been taken to heart by both librarians and bookstore employees, who were recommending it to their customers. (At the end of 1988, the novel would win the American Library Association Award.) She was asked to do interviews; she was asked to write reviews of other books. The temptation of reviewing for *The New York Times Book Review* finally caused her to accept its invitation to write about Clyde Edgerton's recent (Southern) novel. (Kingsolver, *New York Times Book Review,* 10) She was too busy to write seriously.

One kind of climax to the fanfare that was greeting *The Bean Trees* came when people in Carlisle invited her back home for a book-signing. Even though Kingsolver had written a lot about the importance of home and home cultures, it had been some years since she had gone back to Kentucky. Returning would allow her to show off her toddler, Camille, as well as her novel. So in November of 1988, after much of the media attention was over, *The Bean Trees* had its most nostalgic book-signing party.

The small town of 1,600 people closed down so that everyone who wanted to could go to the train depot where Kingsolver would be signing the novel. (*High Tide,* 39) She noted with surprise that all those people paid $16.95 for copies of *The Bean Trees*—and they all wanted to talk about whether or not they were characters in the book. "The county's elected officials" bought the book, she reports, as well as "[m]y first grade teacher, Miss Louella, telling everyone she taught me to write." (39) The crowd even included some of the boys from her high school who had been too disdainful of her skinny smartness to date her.

The fact that her town wanted to do this for her made her realize what a homebody she was—Carlisle, Kentucky, chosen once as "All Kentucky City," was truly important to Barbara Kingsolver, novelist. She reminisced, "Growing up in small town Kentucky taught me respect for the astounding resources people can drum up from their backyards, when they want to, to pull each other through. I tend to be at home with modesty, and suspicious of anything slick or new." (38)

Now thinking about elements of her life from the perspective of a writer, Kingsolver spoke about "accessibility": "I wanted to write a book that my family or my neighbors or the guy that runs Rex and Paul's Service Station ... could read." (Perry interview, 153) She made this decision not only to sell books, but because finding themselves in books made people feel important—which they are. "These people matter. I believe that everything you write is a stream feeding the lake. People like this are worth writing about. People whose main concerns are not the meaning of life necessarily, but, 'Who's going to take care of my kid?'" (152)

CHAPTER SEVEN

The World of
Animal Dreams

Kingsolver is a writer of rare ambition and unequivocal talent ... Animal Dreams *is a complex, passionate, bravely challenging book.*

—*Chicago Tribune*

"I CELEBRATE DEPENDENCY," Kingsolver said in an interview after her first two novels, *The Bean Trees* and *Animal Dreams*, were compared and contrasted. (Perry interview, 146) The two works were seemingly different from each other in many ways. The writer had put herself through the process of shucking off the more visible characteristics of her first novel; she did not want to be the charming Southern voice of a spunky woman like Taylor Greer. Or, rather, she did not want to be *only* that voice.

Barbara Kingsolver, biologist, had come more visibly into the mix of voices as *Animal Dreams* was being conceived and written during late 1988 and 1989. (It was published in 1990, keeping HarperCollins happy for three years in a row—*Homeland and Other Stories* had sold well in 1989, and *The Bean Trees* continued to sell.) The darker tones of the biological processes of both human and animal life surface in her comment later in that same interview that "everything kills something else in order to live." (146) What was hardest for her readers to accept was her equation of human beings with animals, even though, for Kingsolver, such an equation was never negative. It was, simply, realistic.

With *Animal Dreams*, Kingsolver set herself the problem of placing a human family, the Nolines, in the evocative Arizona landscape: she made the human and the animal coalesce. But as she drew the village of Grace, Arizona, with its mixed Spanish, Mexican, and Native American population, she did not sentimentalize the power of community. By making the doctor, Homer Noline, stand outside the culture, saying that he and his people came from Illinois, she isolated her protagonist family and left them outside the circles of fellowship in Grace.

Kingsolver has frequently said that she writes a novel as if she were a scientist: she writes to explore a large philosophical question. "I start every book, every novel, with a question that I can't answer. And my hope, and what keeps it interesting for me, is that I'll write my way to an answer. It has to be an important question[,] ... a question worthy of service of a year or two of my life." (Beattie, ed., 164) *Animal Dreams* interrogates one large question—what the classifications *human* and *animal* mean; but within the human sphere, Kingsolver is intrigued by the problem of how two sisters, reared by the same family, could turn out to be so different. The two daughters of Homer Noline, Halimeda ("Hallie") and Cosima ("Codi") are opposites in their need to explore and interact with the world. It is Hallie who leaves for strife-torn Nicaragua, to help there as an agricultural worker and teacher. She exists in the novel through her letters back to Codi, and through the memories of both her older sister and her slowly deteriorating father. Kingsolver explains:

> When I began to write the story I understood it was a triangle of Codi, Hallie, and Doc Homer, and it was going to be about the ways that memory creates a family and creates a culture.... Hallie would have been very easy because Hallie is me.... Codi's motivations mystified me, and her personality scared me because she's so detached; she's so wounded and she's so cynical.... I didn't like Codi much, and I didn't want to get close to her. (Perry interview, 159–160)

Rather than describing her choice of points of view as a matter of strictly technical concerns, Kingsolver admits that writing in Hallie's voice would have been easy: she understood the character of Hallie. But she wanted to avoid doing another novel written in the first person. Because she knew that Codi was, for her, the problematic consciousness, she created the two-part narrative—Dr. Noline's voice, immersed in long-term memories as his Alzheimer's illness takes over, juxtaposed with Codi's narration. In the process of writing Codi, Kingsolver came to understand her.

The focus question of *Animal Dreams*, then, once the matter of point of view was settled, was:

> Why is it that some people are activists who embrace the world and its problems and feel not only that they can, but that they must, do something about the world and its problems, while other people turn their back on that same world and pretend that it has no bearing on their lives? Why is it, moreover, that these two kinds of people can occur in the same family? (Beattie, ed., 164)

Some of Kingsolver's best writing early in the novel occurs as she charts the sisters' differences. Codi thinks about Hallie:

> She might as well not have had skin, where emotions were concerned. Other people's hurt ran right over into her flesh. For example: I'll flip through a newspaper and take note of the various disasters, and then Hallie will read the same paper and cry her eyes out. She'll feel like she has to do something about it.... [W]here pain seemed to have anesthetized me, it gave Hallie extra nerve endings. (Kingsolver, *Animal Dreams*, 88–89)

In searching for the root of the sisters' difference, Kingsolver came to appreciate the power of memory, which re-constructs past events within the human mind, as well as the power of event itself. The history she gives the Noline daughters is one of the avenues to the richness of the Arizona, and the American, culture. Even if they were separate from the culture, both Hallie and Codi were accepted by the citizens (who knew, in fact, that they were also "family") and thereby given the support of the community.

The daughters grew, however; and they left Grace. (Kingsolver's naming of the town is meant to symbolize the positive power of community.) After Codi's decade of training to be a physician, but not finishing that training; of working inferior jobs; of taking up with men who are not suitable for her; of living a visibly aimless life, she returns to Grace in order to help care for her sick father. It is in the story of her adjusting to Grace, of accepting her friends there, and of learning to understand her seemingly impassive father that the heart of *Animal Dreams* occurs—but it remains a book more about the past than about the immediate present.

Reviewers appreciated its difference from *The Bean Trees*, a novel which—in comparison with *Animal Dreams*—seemed casual, effortless, and perhaps less effective. Taylor Greer enacted her life as it was handed to her: there was no real adversary, there were few choices of conscience or morality. But Codi in *Animal Dreams* has to fight through each decision, has to herself go through the process the novel is undertaking, of ferreting out why she feels as she does. A difficult person faced with a difficult life, Codi Noline is no easy protagonist. It was readers' recognition that Kingsolver's novel did represent this difficult character accurately that informed the reviews; the book was called "an emotional masterpiece," (*New York Daily News*, 1990) "a fully realized and profoundly moral vision," (Holt, 1) and—again, in the earliest full review in *Publishers Weekly*—"[a] well-nigh perfect novel, masterfully written, brimming with insight, humor, and compassion." (*Publishers Weekly*, 1990, 45) That review went on to comment about the difficult structure of the book: "Kingsolver's clear, purposeful prose spins the narrative like a spider's web, its interconnected strands gossamer-thin but tensile, strong." (45)

Animal Dreams provokes the reader as well because it asks for an even-handed response to Doc Homer, who in his stoic, icy demeanor has become the epitome of the *isolato*. Because he is a medical man, the fact that he allows his daughter to come close to death without offering the help he could readily have given divides him as far from the reader as from Codi; in her narrative, Doc

Homer is damned by "his slavish self-sufficiency." His wife's death soon after Hallie's birth leaves his daughters totally dependent on him for everything, including the affection which he withholds.

The book also provokes the reader by asking responses to a number of ecological problems within the Arizona terrain. As Kingsolver draws on what she had learned in covering the Phelps Dodge strike, she gives the area the same bleak promise in the aftermath of decades of mining by the Black Mountain Company that Ajo, Douglas, and Clifton had experienced. The orchards of pecan, plum, and apple are being poisoned out of existence by the sulfuric acid used in Black Mountain's leaching operations. To counter the power of the mine company, she creates a group of tough-minded older women (among the Stitch and Bitch club members, Uda Ruth Dell and Viola Domingos) who take it upon themselves to unsettle the industrialists, the wealthy mine owners, and the gendered culture. In *Animal Dreams*, Kingsolver re-creates the women of *Holding the Line*, and in Codi's involvement with them, using her authority as medical student who has become the high-school science teacher in Grace, she begins to find her way back to humanity. These women, and this secondary plot, provide some relief from the dark recesses of both Doc Homer's wandering memory and the experiences of the daughters' childhood and adolescence.

The Native American character who rescues Codi from her own personal alienation is, like her girlhood friend, Emelina, another way of reaching the human. Loyd Peregrina, a Pueblo, lives by the tenets of his mother's people—those of his Navajo relatives. After he gives up cockfighting, a sport the love of which he had inherited from his long-absent father, he takes Codi to meet his family on the reservation. His definition of home, and his concepts of human happiness, echo Hallie's principles in her letters from Nicaragua. She writes to Codi, "What keeps you going isn't some fine destination but just the road you're on, and the fact that you know how to drive." The disillusionment and angst that mark Codi's response to life have no place in an active, and involved, participatory life. Loyd's definition is brusque: "The important thing isn't the house. It's the ability to make it. You carry that in your brain and in your hands, wherever you go." Codi silently rejoins, "[M]orality is not a large, constructed thing you have or have not, but simply a capacity. Something you carry with you in your brain and in your hands."

Leavened with the heart-stopping beauty of the deer dance, of the millennia-old pueblos, of the unpoisoned natural farms, the discourse between the meaninglessly intellectual Codi and the wise, yet proud, Loyd draws the reader further and further into the distinction, which the novel shows to be arbitrary, between human and animal. The novel opens with Doc Homer watching his children sleep, and equating them with animals: "His girls are curled together like animals whose habit is to sleep underground." In the assessment of critic Janet Bowdan, one of Kingsolver's real strengths as writer is her ability to fuse all parts of a novel. Bowdan notes, "Kingsolver uses boundaries but refuses to maintain all of them at all times: the results create new images, overlapping, demanding inquiry into the idea of possession, position, the habitation of a place, a body, a language." (Bowdan, 16)

A polished structure of complex happenings, *Animal Dreams* seemed much more political than Kingsolver's first several books: readers were somewhat surprised at the intensity of what they named its politics. In Kingsolver's mind, however, *Animal Dreams* was no more political a book than *The Bean Trees* had been. Her first novel had been filled with the issues of child abuse, the Sanctuary movement, the rights of Native American cultures, poverty, and single women as heads of household; *Animal Dreams* probed values of class, especially in mixed-race cultures, where any kind of training or college was scarce; and it extended Kingsolver's interest in matriarchies, particularly within Spanish and Native American cultures. Thematically, it dealt with the losses of a mother and an unborn child, and the effect of those losses on a developing psyche. Its topics included a people's strike against a large mining corporation; trying to repair the ravages of destructive mining practices; and—most dramatically of all—the United States' involvement in a sinister Nicaraguan dictatorship. Yet the political content of these novels received scant mention in the enthusiastic reviews. Only Jane Smiley, in *The New York Times*

Book Review, commented that attempting political expose was difficult; she wrote how hard it is "to forge a compelling political vision in our new world, where so many systems of social organization have turned out to be either ineffectual or bankrupt." (Smiley, 2)

Reflecting later on her books' popularity, Kingsolver commented in the *Progressive* interview, "[I]t has worried me at times that my work is so popular. Sometimes I think, 'Are they just reading the love story and didn't notice the part about Guatemala?'" (Epstein interview, 36) Upon publication, however, much of the success of Kingsolver's novels stemmed from their optimism, their normality, their re-creation of what readers thought was real existence. Admitting that *Animal Dreams* had been a painful novel to write, one that she had revised and revised, Kingsolver felt that the violence and death that occurred in it were necessary. Never a Hollywood version of the random violence of life, her fiction tried to make the point that actions have consequences, and that life will never work if everyone abdicates personal responsibility.

Animal Dreams won the American Library Association Award, just as *The Bean Trees* had. It also won a PEN fiction award and the Edward Abbey Ecofiction Award; and it was nominated for a number of other awards. As Kingsolver's second novel, it brought her even greater praise for her writing, and for her ability to create plausible fictional worlds.

In her strident assessment of what was happening in Nicaragua, however, Kingsolver did not mince emotional truth. She'd dedicated *Animal Dreams* to Ben Linder, the Oregon engineering student who, while helping to build a hydroelectric dam in Nicaragua, had been shot in the head by Contras. (Beattie, ed., 157) She saw more and more signs that the often-praised American democracy was developing an opportunistic underbelly; the profit motive was justifying all kinds of unbelievable alliances. The Persian Gulf War and the political action leading up to it had aroused Kingsolver in ways reminiscent of the years she spent in college protesting the United States choices during the Vietnam conflict: taking her daughter, she lived quietly, modestly, for some months in the Canary Islands. She needed to separate herself from a government that seemed intent on offending her.

When she returned, ready to polish her poem collection for Seal Press and ready to think about her next novel, she was more tranquil: she had realized that there were more than one America. Her poem collection, comprising poems in both an English version and a Spanish translation, was titled *Another America/Otra America*. In readying this poem collection, Kingsolver was surprised at how intimate many of the poems were:

> Writing [poems] felt like a release of the enormous emotional pressuring of those events. Poetry is not for me an intentional thing; I don't plan it, it just happens. It's very different from my fiction. I approach fiction pretty architecturally: I work out the foundations and I build it. (Pence interview, 19)

Another America/Otra America benefited by printing side by side Kingsolver's English poem and Rebeca Cartes' Spanish translation of the same poem. Its divisions within the work emphasize the thematic divisions. Part I, "The House Divided," includes poems about the Gulf War—such as "Deadline" (dated January 15, 1991), in which the poet, standing in protest with her three-year-old daughter, muses, "It has taken your whole self / to bring her undamaged to this moment...." (*Another America*, 5)—and the memory of earlier wars ("Waiting for the Invasion"), as well as poems about the abuse of women. ("Street Scenes," "Reveille") In Part II, "The Visitors," Kingsolver groups most of her poems about refugees—those from Central America whom the Sanctuary movement helped, and others who were denied justice ("Refuge," "In Exile," "Escape," "The Monster's Belly," "For Sacco and Vanzetti").

Her statements about political abuse lead to Part III, titled simply "The Lost." Here is Kingsolver's "American Biographies," an oblique poem about a rape victim; followed by "This House I Cannot Leave" and the related "Ten Forty-Four," the police code for breaking and entering and rape. In this group of three strong poems, Kingsolver suggests that writing about the risks a woman faces is difficult because "the United States is a culture that regards its victims harshly." (Perry interview, 163) With a reference to Anita Hill, Kingsolver continues her explanation of being a rape survivor:

> A lot of women do everything their mothers told them and they still get raped. Anita Hill did everything she was supposed to do and she was still sexually harassed. People don't believe her because they want to believe that if it happened she caused it in some way or another. We can only counter that myth by going public. (Pence interview, 20)

The very act of going public, of writing about rape, abuse, or politics, can stigmatize the writer, however. Readers often dislike anger in poems, even as those works convey "moments of truth." (Perry interview, 162) Kingsolver explains, "The hard part is anticipating the response of a culture that believes victims deserve their fate. I don't believe that I got raped because I asked for it, but...." (164)

In the section "The Lost" the poet also includes moving poems about suicide ("For Richard After All") and mental illness ("Family Secrets") and describes the surrealness of physical loss ("The Loss of My Arms and Legs").

At Part IV, "The Believers," the collection turns. Here Kingsolver shapes the "other" America, the one to which she returned after the Gulf War had ended: "Hope is a renewable option. There is a lot to love here." (160) Her poem "Naming Myself" wrests power out of both silence and anonymity. Recalling her Cherokee great-great-grandmother, the poet writes

> I never knew the grandmother.
> Her photograph has ink-thin braids
> and buttoned clothes, and nothing that she was called
>
> (*Another America*, 61)

"Apotheosis" yearns for the simplicity of a chicken's life; "Orang-Outang" and "Bridges" approach natural law from different points of view. Two birth poems, "Ordinary Miracle" and "Babyblues,"

greet Kingsolver's second daughter; several poems form a brief pro-
thalamion ("Daily Bread," "Watershed," "Possession," "Frankfurt
Cemetery"); and the last poem in the section, "Poem for a Dead
Neighbor," is a commemoration.

Kingsolver's personal balancing act is maintained through this
long and impressive section; Part V, "The Patriots," extends the
comfort of balance into the wider political realm. Kingsolver
opens "The Patriots" with a few lines from Carolyn Forche's *The
Country Between Us*: "It is either the beginning or the end of the
world, and the choice is ourselves or nothing."

The larger causes, like the more intimate ones, fail without a
person's commitment, and the constant search for balance.
Returning to the Nicaraguans dead at the hands of the Contras is
"Our Father Who Drowns the Birds," with its quietly paced,
psalm-like opening:

> There is a season when all wars end:
> when the rains come.
> When the landscape opens its own eyes
> and laughs at your talk of dying.
> When all the dead trees
> open their hands
> to the sky
> and bleed scarlet flowers
> from their fingertips,
> and then you remember, before the blood,
> red was the color you loved.
>
> *(Another America,* 87)

While "The Blood Returns," "The Middle Daughter," and "Your
Mother's Eyes" reinforce the themes of aspects of war and its dam-
ages, Kingsolver's abrupt "On the Morning I Discovered My
Phone Was Tapped" brings the external political world home. So
too does the poem "The Blood Returns," as it testifies to the cyclic
natures of belief and distrust. "Remember the Moon Survives" is a
paean to the cyclic, and to survival. Surviving for Barbara Kingsolver, writer and mother, meant leaving the Canary Islands to

return to the States, to the Arizona that nurtured her life and her daughter's. But as she was to note in "Letter to My Mother," the chilling seeds of separation had already been sown: "[M]y marriage is slowly dying, and I will soon be on my own again[,] ... a single mother." (*Small Wonder*, 172) Kingsolver's prediction was accurate. As never before in her life, she would learn the value of depending on others.

CHAPTER EIGHT

Pigs in Heaven

*Possessed of an extravagantly gifted narrative voice,
Kingsolver blends a fierce and abiding moral vision
with benevolent, concise humor. Her medicine is
meant for the head, the heart, and the soul.*

—*New York Times Book Review*

SOMEHOW, OUT OF THE DEBACLE that her personal life had
become during the separation and eventual divorce, Kingsolver
wrote another successful novel—a true bestseller. Published in
1993 by her usual publisher, HarperCollins, *Pigs in Heaven* had
unpredictably good sales. In it, Kingsolver had returned to the
story of Turtle and Taylor Greer, although she had never expected
to do so.

What had happened was this: Since the 1988 publication of
The Bean Trees, Kingsolver had been flooded with requests that she
continue the story. Few characters had made such an impact on
readers; by the mid-1990s *The Bean Trees* had never gone out of
print. Even more impressive is the fact that Kingsolver's first novel
was available for purchase in sixty-five countries. (Annenberg film)

Another, more critical, piece of the situation was the fact that
Kingsolver had come to understand that in *The Bean Trees* she had
ignorantly persuaded her readers to hope that Turtle would escape

her Indian culture. She had not learned about the 1978 Indian Child Welfare Act until long after *The Bean Trees* had been published; once she became informed, however, she saw a way to make amends for Taylor's duplicity in her adoption of Turtle. In her second novel about them, the claims of the Indian community would be heard sympathetically. As she explained, "I realized with embarrassment that I had completely neglected a whole moral area." (Perry interview, 165)

When Kingsolver discusses *Pigs in Heaven*, she describes it as a novel that grew, in large part, out of Arizona news. A white couple in South Tucson had informally adopted a Native American child. When the tribe demanded that the child be returned, all public sympathy was given to the white foster mother. What intrigued Kingsolver was the fact that neither side could hear the demands of the other: "[I]n the mainstream Anglo-Saxon society, ... our fundamental unit of good is the individual, is what is best for the individual.... [I]n the tribe, the fundamental unit of good is what's good for the community." (Beattie, ed., 170) Because the assumptions are so different, no one can see any way to compromise.

What Kingsolver found was that readers did instinctively want to keep a child with a mother. No simple presentation of fact or law was going to make the Indian point of view appealing. What the dilemma meant for *Pigs in Heaven* was that the story of Turtle and Taylor Greer barely opened before it was buried beneath a series of extended dialogues. After the protagonists have appeared on *The Oprah Winfrey Show* (because Turtle has been credited with saving a man's life), Annawake Fourkiller, a young Indian lawyer, comes to question Taylor. Her conversations with first Taylor and then Jax, Taylor's musician boyfriend, and later with Alice, Taylor's mother, provide much of the legal and historical background. Slow reading, these discussions are somewhat palatable because the reader already knows that Turtle and Taylor may be in serious trouble; what suspense exists continues on from the plot of *The Bean Trees*.

Kingsolver tries to make the Indian point of view credible by drawing Annawake as both beautiful and committed to justice for all Indian children. Her twin brother's adoption out of the tribe after their mother's institutionalization had brought her deep sorrow; many of her responses are more emotional than legalistic. It is Annawake who supplies the novel's title as she tells Alice about the Native American belief that six bad pigs constitute the Pleiades (in contrast with the occidental legend of the Seven Sisters). The Indian explanation for the star formation is that six Indian boys defied the wishes of their mothers and refused to work; the mothers then fed them food fit only for pigs. They were changed into pigs—even as their mothers chased them up into the sky, bargaining with the spirits to have their sons returned.

Alice is moved by the story:

> "Law.... They must of felt awful." "They did. They tried to grab their sons by the tails, and they begged the spirits to bring them back, but it was too late. The pigs ran so fast they were just a blur, and they started rising up into the sky. The spirits put them up there to stay. To remind parents always to love their kids no matter what, I guess, and cut them a little slack."

> Alice looks up for a long time. "I swear there's seven," she says.

> The owl hoots again, nearer this time.

> "Maybe so," Annawake says. "The Six Pigs in Heaven, and the one mother who wouldn't let go."
>
> (Kingsolver, *Pigs in Heaven*, 314)

Part of the vitality of the novel stems from the language of its women characters, and the book reads in its quiet way as a celebration of the communities of women who can stand by one another. But that emphasis is more subtle in this novel.

Kingsolver's lead question for *Pigs in Heaven*, then, remained, "In this dialogue, is there any point of intersection?" (Beattie, ed., 170) Getting at the distinction between the individual and the community, Kingsolver also worked hard to write the book in the third person, rather than in any combinations of the first person, so that she could "give absolutely equal weight and moral authority to both Taylor's point of view and the tribe's." (170) In this novel, perhaps more visibly than in her first two books, Kingsolver's aim to promote "social justice" underlay much of the story. (Annenberg film)

Difficult for Kingsolver to write with the kind of passion she usually displayed, this narrative gave her "knots" in her stomach because she saw no possible compromise. (Perry interview, 164) As she explained, "In all my other books the villain is offstage: it's the community against the bad mining company or it's the women against poverty...." In *Pigs in Heaven,* the conflict was between two well-drawn, interesting women characters—and their point of argumentation was the proprietorship of the innocent child, Turtle Greer. Noting that her HarperCollins editor had pointed out that she herself tended to avoid conflict, Kingsolver agreed: "You know, raise your voice and I'll be under the desk in an instant.... It was very hard for me to write about direct conflict between characters." (Beattie, ed., 170)

One of the ways she avoided much of the conflict was to have Taylor spirit Turtle away. If the jurisdiction of the Cherokee tribe was one of the problems, they would relocate. The absence of the two as they tried to establish a life for themselves in Seattle, Washington, hurt the novel. But in that vacuum, Kingsolver developed the persona of Taylor's mother, Alice Greer, a wonderfully plausible older character.

The novel begins with a chapter about Alice, married for the past two years, for the second time, to a man who is not, after all, ideal. Kingsolver notes, "This marriage has failed to warm her"; given the fact that Alice had been single for long years, she was not ready to settle for less than good. Alice describes talking with Harland as "like trying to have a conversation with a ironing board." At sixty-one, Alice is independent, loving, and aware of her own sexuality: she is not a Mattie figure, self-sacrificing or involved primarily in a social cause. She is an older version of Taylor.

The second way in which *Pigs in Heaven* differs from both *The Bean Trees* and *Animal Dreams* is that it makes a point of Taylor's financial inability to live on her own. Once she moves to Seattle, where she knows nobody and has no childcare for Turtle, she understands that she cannot make it. The problem is one of simple dollars and cents. As her mother reports after a phone call, "Last time I talked to her she didn't sound like herself. She's depressed. It's awful what happens when people run out of money. They start thinking they're no good." The jobs she is able to get are lost when she has inadequate childcare; most of her pay goes for rent. And, as Alice continues, "Taylor just bought new school clothes for Turtle instead of paying her bills. She was scared to death of Turtle looking poor at school. You know how it is."

Taking up one of the oldest of America's myths, that of Horatio Alger, the poor newsboy who succeeds by becoming wealthy, Kingsolver has challenged the belief that "anyone can make it in America if you're smart and work hard." "Well," she asks, "for how many generations now has that been untrue? ... [M]y generation is not as well off as our parents, even though we worked just as hard, and more of us got more of an education than they had." (Epstein interview, 36) To be poor is to have failed. To be female and have a child or children to care for is to struggle against nearly impossible odds. In *The Bean Trees*, the support of Mattie (in giving Taylor a job), Lou Ann (in sharing her house), and other women in the community obviated the discussion of poverty; in *Animal Dreams*, Codi returned to her father's community, lived with her best friend's family, and was hired quickly by the public school system. Again, poverty afflicts other characters in the narrative but not the protagonist.

In *Pigs in Heaven*, in contrast, Taylor's flight in order to keep Turtle only puts her at great risk of losing the child. As she explains to Jax when he calls her from a pay phone in Seattle—the poor have no phones in their rentals, nor do they have ATM cards or checking accounts—"I can't believe how bad I've screwed up here. I lost the van-driving job. I couldn't work out the baby-sitting." Now making six dollars an hour in a department store, she finds her paycheck reduced by "taxes and Social Security and this mandatory insurance plan that I can't even use yet for six months." She tells him her expenses: after rent and utilities, "another fifty a month to keep the car going so I can get to work. If we can get by on a hundred a month for food, that should leave fifty dollars for emergencies. But Jax, we just keep getting behind. I had a car-insurance payment come due." At his urging that he borrow money and send her plane tickets to come home, she insists that she has to do this on her own. But she admits, "[I]t was different there, with you and me to split the rent, and Lou Ann always around for baby-sitting."

In *Pigs in Heaven*, a kind of larger responsibility overshadows romance. Without any visible support, Alice leaves Harland; and while Taylor finds that she does love Jax and wants to return to him, her life is also based on friendships and her love for both her mother and Turtle. The novel's principles are in keeping with Kingsolver's own belief system: "Most of my life is about connect-edness, and it's about community. I want people to believe that kind of stuff is worthy of literature." (Pence interview, 20)

The focus for the community efforts, in *Pigs in Heaven* as in *The Bean Trees*, is Turtle and her well-being. Signaled by the devel-opment of her idiosyncratic vegetable-based language in the first novel, her increasingly full response to Taylor—and to Lou Ann and Alice and Mattie and Jax—in the second book is described as her recovery of memory. The burial of her mother surfaces repeat-edly in Turtle's timid fascination with cemeteries and in her attempts to dig holes and place objects under the earth; just as Kingsolver questioned the literal definitions of *home* and *family*, and *animal* and *human*, she makes the reader conscious of the fact that to *bury* (or *plant*) may result in *growth* and *fruition*. Turtle's life has come to illustrate that flowering. And in *Pigs in Heaven*, the contrived yet satisfactory ending is helped in its resolution because Turtle/Lacey remembers the identity of her long-lost "good" grandfather. Memory, too, helps a life grow.

Contrary to most reviews of the novel, finally, a good bit of the plot of *Pigs in Heaven* had little to do with Native American cul-ture, and Kingsolver spoke to that fact when she said that the novel's focus was on the philosophical dimensions of these charac-ters' lives, lives that might suggest wide applications of the events for her readers. She said in her *Progressive* interview, "What I really wanted to do in that book was not necessarily write about Indians. I wanted to introduce my readers to this completely different unit of good and have them believe in it by the end, have them accept in their hearts that that could be just as true as the other."(Epstein interview, 37)

Perhaps some of Kingsolver's emphasis on the desperate financial situation Taylor finds herself in reflected her own unpreparedness for being a single parent. As she wrote several years after her divorce:

> '92 was a rotten year. My marriage of many years had been transferred suddenly from the intensive care ward to the autopsy table. I was single ... and reeling between shock and despair.... I was completely overwhelmed with the tasks of being mother of a preschooler, full-time author with big deadlines, carpool driver, chief cook, good citizen, breadwinner, and fixer of all broken things around the house." (Kingsolver, *Mid-Life Confidential*, 197)

With her characteristic reasonable humor, however, she continues, "The key to survival is something called 'multitasking.' You figure out how to combine compatible chores: phone consultations with your editor and washing the breakfast dishes. Writing a novel in the pediatrician's waiting room. Grocery shopping and teaching your child to read. Sleeping and worrying. Sobbing and driving." (197)

There is the financial devastation of single parenthood, but there is also—probably worse—the emotional devastation. Loneliness is multiplied exponentially when one is faced with not only individual aloneness but the unremitting care of children. Suddenly the comfort of the implicit support of being one of *two* parents disappears: the single parent, in effect, makes all the decisions, from tiny to huge.

Seeing and hearing the true state of Kingsolver's emotional health after her return from the Canary Islands, her agent and friends at HarperCollins insisted that she take advantage of the perquisites of being an established author: she must accept an invitation to visit Japan, she must become involved in the authors' rock band planned for a May, 1992, performance at the American Book Sellers Association convention, and, in 1993, she must do a book tour for *Pigs in Heaven*. Unlike most successful novelists, Kingsolver had never done any kind of promotional tour. Harper-Collins knew how profitable "city-a-day" travel could be; they insisted that she participate in the extensive planning for the post-publication undertaking. (Of course, first she needed to finish writing the manuscript that would become *Pigs in Heaven*.)

If 1992 was by her own admission a nearly unbearable year, the resonating bright spot in it was the May 25 performance of the Rock Bottom Remainders, with two shows scheduled at a night-club called Cowboy Boogie in Anaheim, California. The brainchild of Kathi Goldmark, the group included Stephen King; Roy Blount, Jr.; Ridley Pearson; Amy Tan; Dave Barry; Tad Bartimus; and others, under the informal direction of Al Kooper. Lured into the project largely because she had been out of the States, Kingsolver was surprised when she returned to find much correspondence—both letters and faxes—about the rock group. She felt as if she needed to be a member, especially because they seemed to have no other keyboard player.

Her decision was important for two reasons. First, it brought her back into the world of music, for which she'd had too little time since 1987, when her daughter was born, followed in 1988 by the publication of *The Bean Trees*. As Kingsolver wrote in her essay about the rock group:

> For all the years I've worked as a writer, I've also played piano and synthesizer, bass clarinet, guitar, and lately even conga drums. I have sung in the shower. (I sound great in the shower.) I have howled backup to Annie Lennox and Randy Travis and Rory Block in my car. I've played in garage bands and jammed informally with musician friends, and with them have even written and recorded a few original songs.... (*Mid-Life*, 200)

Her discussion in the essay is contextualized by her comments that she has always been too diverse—"A business card that lists more than one profession does not go down well in the grownup set"—that she wanted to be too many things. She has *always* wanted to be too many things.

What she brought to the Rock Bottom Remainders, accordingly, was her best effort. In that, she was like each member of the group—not one of them was content to just show up. In their attempts to make the group work, necessarily, real friendships grew. (Wagner-Martin interview) And also, perhaps necessarily, one performance was not enough. After the May 1992 show, plans were made for a two-week tour during May of 1993. (The essays in *Mid-Life Confidential* grew out of that saga.)

Unsure that she could spare the two weeks for the practices in Boston and then the tour itself down the East coast to conclude in Miami, Kingsolver was surprised at her friends' urging: "Tad and Ridley and Amy called me up to tell me I needed to have some fun. Steve King sent so many mailgrams, I became a cult figure at my post office." (*Mid-Life*, 198) And on her birthday, when she had returned from a long walk, she found messages from everyone on her answering machine.

So she was in. Everyone in the group had spent the year practicing; they were much better. As a paragraph in her novel *Pigs in Heaven* showed, Kingsolver, speaking through Jax the musician, felt herself back in touch with her instrument. Jax is taking apart the keyboard to clean it: "It always amazes him: it can produce sounds exactly like a piano, a Hammond organ, a muted French horn, even breaking glass or a marble rolling down the inside of a pipe, and yet there is practically nothing inside." (*Pigs in Heaven*, 242) The musician and the instrument: a pair, something like the horse and his jockey, or the parent and the child. Each of them shared that love of their instrument. Kingsolver remembered, "The truth is, in rehearsal we all paid attention.... I tried to be dependable and invisible and watch my little buttons so I didn't come in sounding like a horn section when I was supposed to be an organ, or vice versa.... I wanted to belong to this gang." (*Mid-Life*, 198)

The second reason why her participation in the Rock Bottom Remainders was crucial was exactly that—belonging. The writer's life, both in writing and in book touring, is spent entirely alone. (In Kingsolver's language, "Book tours are as lonely as a prison term.... [W]hat they don't offer is the chance to belong to a group.") (202) The appeal of the group was its camaraderie—talented and nice people working toward something they were not sure they could achieve—everyone helping each other, gaining confidence from the successes, growing. Kingsolver wrote in her essay about the Remainders:

> There is a kind of veracity of experience that only comes—to me, anyway—from seeing my own delight reflected in someone else's eyes. That was the thrill of the Rock Bottom Remainders. I must have sought it out in the middle of my dark winter, like a pale seedling straining for sun, because somewhere in the basement of my boarded-up heart I knew it was what I needed. Tad's enormous eyes, wide and starry with mascara, smiling at mine in the dressing room mirror as we prayed we'd hit our notes. Amy with her chin tipped up, glancing over for her cue on "Leader of the Pack." Steve's little wink when he takes over the whistle reprise on "Dock of the Bay." Dave's grin and Ridley's smiling nod as we look at each other and move, smooth as silk, from A major into the F-sharp-minor bridge that we always screwed up in rehearsal. Look at us, we are saying to each other. This is really happening.... (203)

CHAPTER NINE

New Beginnings,
New Books

I would have to say I'm a storyteller. Everything I write is a story. My novels are long stories or bunches of stories all kind of bound together at the center with twine. My short stories are stories. My poems are little true stories, sort of emotionally intense stories. My nonfiction is always stories. Even when I do some travel writing for the New York Times, what I find is I can't write a regular, straight travel article.... I have to write a story.

—Barbara Kingsolver, *Kentucky Writers*

A THOROUGHLY PROFESSIONAL WOMAN, Barbara Kingsolver is known to her friends and her publishers as one who keeps on going. To her new buddies among the Remainders, she was also quietly beloved: Kathi Goldmark remembers her "humor, integrity, and musicianship," (*Mid-Life*, 56) Tad Bartimus, her "warm greeting ... leavened with humor and curiosity." (158) Joel Selwin thought she was "probably the most gifted musician in the lot." (102) In Ridley Pearson's description comes the sense of the niceness, the professionalism, and—at this time—the underlying strain:

> Pushed by her publisher to be six places at once. Intellectual. Studied. Like me, she's thrown off when Al [Kooper] abruptly changes the parts she has studied and learned so diligently. Uncomfortable with this whole *idea*, but reluctantly accepts her commitment and therefore tears into it.... Private. Reserved. Nothing to prove. Nice smile, and uses it freely. Says a lot with her eyes across stage, like: "What's the next chord?" (77)

The fact that people liked and admired her didn't erase her need to have help. One of the biggest obstacles to becoming a prominent and visible author was childcare. In that respect, her parents in Kentucky were always ready to help—but Arizona was a long way from north-central Kentucky.

She arranged the *Pigs in Heaven* book tour, for example, so that her daughter went with her for the first few days and then stayed with her parents for several weeks, and resumed the tour with her at the end. (Wagner-Martin interview) In Kingsolver's mind, this was an exceptionally long and difficult time of traveling. When she had gone to Japan, she had taken Camille with her; and during the Remainders' tour, she had taken some days off from the middle of the schedule in order to go back to her family. She was learning to multitask, in that when she traveled she wrote essays, shorter pieces that could be marketed separately and would also appear in the collection of essays her agent had asked her to compile for HarperCollins.

Accordingly, when the Lila Wallace Foundation invited her to be visiting writer for a college, she asked that the campus they chose be near her parents' home so that Camille could stay with her grandparents. That was why Kingsolver arrived at the small Virginia school in southern Appalachia to teach both in the English Department and in the Ecology area, and there she met Steven Hopp, the ornithologist and musician who would become her second husband. The two shared a great love for the land, farming, music, people, a pared-down life, and birds and other animals—and they were both political people. Kingsolver wrote about their meeting in the essay "Reprise":

On the day we met, my mate and I, he invited me to take a walk in the wooded hills of his farm.... I told him I loved the woods, and he took my word for that, and headed lickety-split up the mountainside. I ran after, tearing through blackberry briars with the options of getting hopelessly lost or keeping up. He did remember, after all, that I was behind him. When he reached the top of the mountain he waited, and we sat down together on a rock, listening to the stillness in the leaves. (*High Tide*, 268–269)

That essay had begun with the wedding that followed their courtship, a ceremony which took place "in the sight of pine-browed mountains, a forget-me-not sky, and nearly all the people I love most. This is not the end of the story; I know that much. With senseless mad joy, I'm undertaking what Samuel Johnson called the triumph of hope over experience—the second marriage."

A typical Kingsolver essay, "Reprise" draws from the personal, gives the reader the sense of a speaking voice, and expands to include a more abstract moral—in this case, the value of hope. Readers found in Kingsolver's essays many of the qualities that made her fiction so appealing. Regardless of what the essays were about, the author wrote in a recognizable and approachable voice. She believed in stories, so the essay was often organized around a story which began the piece and then concluded it.

The essay collection, *High Tide in Tucson,* also worked in that way. When Kingsolver traveled to the Bahamas, she brought back shells for her daughter. Hidden in one of them was a small crab. Buster, in his aquarium, had then to acclimate to life in the Arizona desert, which he seemed to do by finding a tidal pattern to build his life rhythms around. Kingsolver described the effect:

When Buster is running around for all he's worth, I can only presume it's high tide in Tucson. With or without evidence, I'm romantic enough to believe it. This is the lesson of Buster, the poetry that camps outside the halls of science: Jump for joy, hallelujah. Even a desert has tides. (*High Tide*, 6)

The miracle of the crustacean's adaptability became a metaphor for human indomitability—and hope. "High Tide in Tucson" was the essay about Buster, and it became the title of the book because Kingsolver thought many of her essays were in themselves hopeful.

High Tide in Tucson was a book that, once again, chalked up unusually high sales. Perhaps because it had been two years since Kingsolver had published a book of any kind, or perhaps because some of the essays included had been published in *The New York Times*, readers were eager to buy the hard-cover edition. Such a response was surprising; essay collections are notoriously hard to sell.

It is a substantial book, filled with essays on a variety of topics. Many of them are autobiographical; some are about writing; others are about the author's travels to Africa, Hawaii, the Bahamas; but more are about the ecological concerns relevant to both Kingsolver's home state of Kentucky and her adoptive place, Arizona. Each essay is satisfying in its shape: Kingsolver uses the story-as-beginning and then weaves the essay from that starting point. She also organized the collection to give the reader a sense of progression, saying in the preface that some of the essays "connect with and depend on their predecessors." (*High Tide*, x)

Many of the pieces are moderated to be comic. While the author may not want the world of readers laughing at her somewhat uncaring taste in clothes, she is not above admitting the years she has anguished over her lack of stylishness. In "Life Without Go-Go Boots," she describes being unfashionable in high school but then moves on to the premise that being a writer means she is forever exempt from the dictates of high fashion—or even middle-class fashion. (When an East Coast friend took her shopping for a reasonably chic silk suit, however, the friend admonished her, "Barbara, you're not eccentric, you're an anachronism.") (*High Tide*, 56) In "The Muscle Mystique," she critiques today's cultural concern with "fashionable" bodies; in "The Household Zen," she defends her style of "lick and a promise" house cleaning. (60)

Most of the essays could not be described as comic, of course, but Kingsolver uses humor to leaven even her more serious pieces. The essays about living in the Canary Islands, for example— "Somebody's Baby" and "Paradise Lost"—focus on the fact that "people there like kids," so her identity as the mother of a win-some child was pleasant. (99) She talks about building self-esteem in a child, and uses as an illustration of her own lack of that, the story of her remorse at sixteen when she failed her driving test. But she also segues into the warmth toward children that her family evinced: "My grandfathers on both sides lived in households that were called upon, after tragedy struck close to home, to take in orphaned children and raise them without a thought." (101) These pieces are like "The Vibrations of Djoogbe" and "Infernal Paradise" in that they are more personal than most travel essays.

These essays are connected thematically to "Stone Soup," in which she redefines the family. "Stone Soup" also illustrates another of Kingsolver's effective essay techniques: almost unpre-dictably, she brings into discussions a comment that is very personal, probably autobiographical, and the insertion brings the reader back into the recognition that this *is* Kingsolver's essay, Kingsolver's story. In "Stone Soup," for example, in the midst of somewhat generalized commentary appears this several-sentence unit: "A nonfunctioning marriage is a slow asphyxiation. It is waking up despised each morning, listening to the pulse of your own loneliness...." (138)

Sometimes the insertions are less autobiographical, but they ring true as Kingsolver's opinion—in contrast to the more objec-tive view of Kingsolver the essayist. In "The Spaces Between," an essay largely about the Heard Museum and Native American cul-ture, Kingsolver notes, "[L]ately we've been besieged with a new, bizarre form of racism that sets apart all things Native American as object of either worship or commerce.... What began as anthro-pology has escalated to fad, and it strikes me that assigning magical power to a culture's every belief and by-product is simply another way of setting those people apart." (148)

One of her best essays combines these techniques to create its impact. "The Memory Place" is about her Kentucky homelands. It is also about herself as mother (and daughter), and about the pris-tine imagination of her child. It is one of the earliest of her incipient ecological essays, focusing in detail on the "jigsaw puzzle of public and private property" that is the Kentucky watershed she describes. (177) The essay, for all its practical purposes, is also poetry. It begins:

> This is the kind of April morning no other month can touch: a world tinted in watercolor pastels of redbud, dogtooth violet, and gentle rain. The trees are beginning to shrug off winter; the dark, leggy maple woods are shot through with gleaming constellations of soft white dogwood blossoms. The road winds through deep forest near Cumberland Falls, Kentucky, carrying us across the Cumberland Plateau toward Horse Lick Creek. Camille is quiet beside me in the front seat, until at last she sighs and says, with a child's poetic logic, 'This reminds me of the place I always like to think about.' (170)

Much like her craft in the essays "The Forest in the Seeds" and "In Case You Ever Want to Go Home Again," here Kingsolver beckons the reader into substantive issues even as she seems to be speaking leisurely.

The next three years were given to the immensity of Kingsolver's undertaking her African book. She had made two trips to that continent (although the Congo/Zaire was off limits) during 1992 and 1993; then she had married, and then she and Steven had had a daughter. The family was now establishing their seasonal rhythm: during the school year, they lived in Arizona and grew "broccoli, peas, spinach, lettuce, Chinese vegetables, artichokes" (*Small Wonder*, 116); in the Southern summers, when they moved back to Appalachia, they grew "everything else: corn, peppers, green beans, tomatoes, eggplants, too much zucchini, and never enough of the staples (potatoes, dried beans)." Kingsolver explained calmly, "By turns we work two very different farms." (116)

The 1990s were also busy with plans for the tenth-anniversary publication of *The Bean Trees*, and the Seal Press publication in 1998 of the second edition of *Another America/Otra America*. That press had asked Margaret Randall to write a foreword; Kingsolver also wrote an introduction (she added half a dozen poems, all of which were translated into Spanish), and there too the voice of the essayist spoke clearly. Whereas Kingsolver wrote about the importance of poetry *per se,* Randall wrote about the importance of political poetry.

In the 1998 reissue, Randall lamented today's "times of almost total cynicism" (*Another America,* xi) and rehearsed the more auspicious decades—the 1960s, 1970s, and 1980s—when a poet could be political. She compared Kingsolver's work with that of June Jordan, Alice Walker, Adrienne Rich. Keeping one's belief in either the quest for justice or the power of poetry, she argued, is hard, especially "since the loss of Nicaragua and the very mediated victories in El Salvador, Guatemala, parts of Africa and Asia." (xii) Kingsolver's poems give the reader hope.

For Kingsolver, poetry remains a mystery; it "approaches, pauses, then skirts around us like a cat.... It is elementary grace, communicated from one soul to another.... [I]t sings us awake, it's irresistible, it's congenital." (*Another America,* xvi) And then, in true essayist fashion, she brings her abstract description down to the words of her one-year-old, who "stood on a chair reciting the poems she seems to have brought with her onto this planet." (xvii) Kingsolver writes about her personal need to "howl and cry and laugh" (xix) a poem into existence; and the fact that much of her poetry exists because of the heartlessness of political decisions, the "unspeakable things" that—perhaps with art like the poem—"can be survived."

In some ways, Kingsolver's next projected novel was even more staggering than its subject matter would suggest: it was to be a kind of *double* African novel. One part of the book that became *The Poisonwood Bible* was the actual history of the Congo and its fight for independence in the early 1960s. (As the author thinks about the political trauma of the time, she describes the Congo as a country that "almost had self determination" (Rehm interview) but then it was usurped—by the United States, by the CIA; and the dictator Mobutu Sese Seko was "cheerfully supported by the U.S. for the next thirty years.") As a writer, Kingsolver knew that mere history—no matter how accurate and eventful—was never as remarkable as a fiction dealing with the history. She had told Diane Rehm, "I wanted to tell this political story in a very personal way because that's what a novel can do." While history remains impersonal, the novel lets readers identify: "When you pick up a novel, you put down your own life. The novel is scenic; it describes a world to you through someone who isn't you." (Rehm)

The vehicle for Kingsolver's telling of the Congolese struggle for independence—and its quick extinguishing—became the narrative of the Price family's mission, to go to the Congo in order to Christianize the heathens. Part II of *The Poisonwood Bible*, then, was the dramatic story of the tyrannous Nathan Price, "zealot" and Georgia Baptist minister, and his long-suffering wife, Orleanna, and their four daughters. Orleanna comes to have a dominant place in the telling of the story—"trying to be a good wife, she feels she has no choice." (Rehm) The family, however, "has no idea what they are getting into."

Although her family was nothing like the fictional Price family, the author was drawing in some respects on their months in Africa in 1963, when her father went on a medical mission to the primitive villages. As Kingsolver said, "For about half my life I have wanted to write a novel about and set in Africa, owing to the piece of my childhood that I spent there. And I have written something that feels like the first chapter of that novel ... that I'm finally ready to do that." (Beattie, ed., 171)

Kingsolver's fascination with Africa was not simply personal. From her college days she had been reading Doris Lessing's work, and part of her interest in that writer was the legitimate connection between the personal and the political. She recalled, "I read everything of Lessing's. I loved the way she evoked Africa. But more than that, maybe on a less conscious level, I loved the fact that she was writing about something real and important—the frustration of women who had absolutely no choices in their lives...." (Perry interview, 150) In contrast, as she says on camera, Kingsolver wanted to create fictions where people were able to find, and make, choices: "I want people to be hopeful, to think they can change the world." (Annenberg film)

Writing *The Poisonwood Bible* took years of preparation in libraries as well: "Historical fiction is a frightening labor-intensive proposition.... I read a lot of books about the political, social, and natural history of Africa and the Congo." It was slow work. "Sometimes, reading a whole, densely-written book on, say, the formation and dissolution of indigenous political parties during the Congolese independence, or an account of the life histories of Central African venomous snakes, would move me only a sentence or two forward in my understanding of my subject. But every sentence mattered." (Kingsolver website)

She also read extensively in the King James Bible, feeling for "the rhythm of the Price family's speech, the frame of reference for their beliefs, and countless plot ideas." (website) But most important to her understanding of the Congolese languages, she read "a huge old two-volume Kikongo–French dictionary, compiled early in the century (by a missionary, of course). Slowly I began to grasp the music and subtlety of this amazing African language, with its infinite capacity for being misunderstood and mistranslated." (website)

Kingsolver's title comes from that pattern of misunderstanding. "Poisonwood" (*bangala*) when differently inflected is "Beloved Lord." When Nathan Price thinks he is being his most reverent, he is insulting: his children understand the difference in pronunciation, but since he has never listened to anyone in his life, he remains stubbornly wrong. All the promise of his mission to the Africans disintegrates into the wrong words, spoken in the wrong way. Nathan's whirlwind of error carries him to his ridicule, and his death.

The way in which the author chooses to tell the Price family's story gives her choices that keep readers sheltered for a time from the truth about Nathan's mania. She tells the story through a series of religious metaphors. By opening each of the long narrative's seven books with a Bible verse (or a verse from the Apocrypha), she forces the reader to question the minister's authority. For instance, what is the "pearl of great price" that Nathan Price will trade the safety and well-being of his family to win? The epigraphs to each book move the narrative along, subtly. As epigraph for Book Three, Kingsolver chooses Judges 2:2–3, a passage that speaks directly to the plight of the Congolese in Nathan's hands:

And ye shall make no league with the
inhabitants of this land;
ye shall throw down their altars ...
They shall be as thorns in your sides,
and their gods shall be a snare unto you.

(Kingsolver, *The Poisonwood Bible*, 187)

In trampling the people's beliefs underfoot, the Georgia minister has thrown down the existing altars; he duels with existing gods. He cannot but lose. Taking the Bible and the situation as ironic brings the reader more fully into the passive Orleanna's questioning of Nathan's decisions. It is her heart of darkness that ignites the narrative; she finally has no choice but to recognize her husband's madness, and to leave him.

Kingsolver's narrative technique of using the opening verse as a fulcrum for each book—some of the books nearly a hundred pages long—is more than a tour de force, however. The strategy stems from Nathan's psychosis: his punishment for his daughters, chosen with mean appropriateness, is to assign each of them "the verse." Whenever any of the four displeases him, he chooses one verse. She must then reach that verse by copying out the one hundred verses that precede it—a progression of guilt that finally brings her to the single verse, her father's "word." The words may be from the Bible, but the choice of them—and the emphatic "last word"—is her father's. The punishment is *his*, not God's. Such a travesty of education shows Nathan's need to garner power from all sources. Nathan Price is a spoiler, not a cherisher.

In a style reminiscent of the method William Faulkner used in his novel *As I Lay Dying*, Kingsolver sets up an intricate seven-book structure comprising more than a hundred narrative segments, each spoken by one of the four daughters—Rachel, the oldest; Adah and Leah, the incompatible twins; and Ruth May, the preschooler. One daughter's name appears at the head of every section.

Each of the seven books follows the same structural organization. First comes the Bible verse. After each opening epigraph comes the mother's meditation, a segment that creates a poetic tone and in some cases a key image for the various stories to follow. The innocent wife, who has followed her charismatic, religious spouse into the truly unknown country, serves as an emotional base for the narrative of the sometimes unbelievable events. Nathan Price has no voiced sections of his own; he is seen only through his children's eyes.

The structure of the book creates a story that is more gendered than it might at first appear. While none of the Price family members understands either their endeavor or the culture into which they have come, the women are innocent of any duplicity. All power, and all control, is Nathan's. The Price women are literally without price because, in Nathan's eyes, they are valueless. The indeterminacy within the novel stems from Kingsolver's striking convention of choosing as narrators of the events characters who are, initially, powerless. Each of the daughters grows with the story—although none is able to save the family.

One of the author's skills as novelist lies in her believable differentiation of the four daughters. There is the oldest, Rachel—impatient, vain, and blessed with comic malapropisms (which are not dependent on the difference between Congolese and English). There are the gifted twins Leah and Adah, both trapped—one by disability, the other by pride. And there is the sweet child, Ruth May, the essence of hope. It is she who breaks through the language barrier and teaches the young Africans to play "Mother, May I?" with her and her sisters. Ruth May is the true missionary.

Most of Kingsolver's efforts to have her four narrators grow and change, hopefully becoming responsive to the struggles of the Congo, achieve little visibility. As if continually reminding the reader that little freedom is possible, whether women live in the States or in the Congo, Kingsolver stays within the conventions of women's lives—what are the roles of obedient daughters? What are the roles of obedient wives? One of the reasons the story of the Congolese struggle for independence is so muted in *The Poisonwood Bible* is that any attempt to gain freedom—from any dictator or any patriarch—jars against the submission expected from the family of Nathan Price. To keep the novel in the hands of its human subjects is to keep its emotional tone static.

While the book is overtly political—beginning in 1959 and following the Congo's independence from Belgium through five years of struggle (complete with the stories of Patrice Lumumba, Mobutu, Moise Tshombe, and their partisans)—it remains the story of institutional, religious patriarchy. By combining Nathan Price's authority as husband and father with his less questionable role as religious leader, Kingsolver sets for her readers the same dilemma his wife and daughters face: how to separate Nathan Price, the abusive spouse and parent, from Nathan Price, the minister of God's word.

Using the narrative sections of Leah, the most generous of the daughters, Kingsolver shows the gradual change in the family's perception of Nathan: he devolves from a modest World War II hero (bothered by his unknown "war injury") to "a small befuddled stranger," defeated by his failure to harvest either food or souls in the Congolese climate. As his sometimes hidden rage builds to mind-destroying fury, Nathan unleashes the self-hatred of his irreparable war wound—his guilt at being the one man to live through the brutal devastation of the war. Using Nathan to show the theme of war as wound, and wounding, strengthens Kingsolver's narrative of the Congo's fight for national independence, a fight that will foment destruction. Again, the impersonality of war is vividly translated through the story of the human waste it inevitably creates. As his disillusionment leads to paranoia, he is head of the family in name only.

None of the other characters is able to take over his role. Given their training as submissive girls and women, they have little choice but to run from the mad minister—which they eventually do. Their survival from the warlike conditions of the political uprising, as well as from the inimical jungle, is meant to be read as a miracle. Kingsolver, however, does not mystify the way the various daughters and their mother endure the hardships of running away; each behaves true to the character previously shown through their voices in narration. The reader does not care to exist with Rachel, for example, who is so unaware of politics that she survives by prostituting herself to the wrong side. Adah's survival, which is physically elaborate, involves retraining her disabled body to become more nearly whole: that she becomes a physician, talking her way into Emory University for undergraduate school, is less to her credit than the outcome of her alienated psyche. The reader does not particularly like Adah, either, despite her success within the American economy. And Leah, by succumbing to all the allures of Africa itself, bearing four children to her Congolese husband and relinquishing her life as an American, is also strangely distant from the struggles that marked the entire Price family.

The Poisonwood Bible is not meant to be a happy story. Invested as the reader is in the separate narratives of the four daughters, the movement of the conflicted family into the Congolese culture has a great deal of suspense. But the narrators, like the positive progression of the story, run short: they are not super heroes, their stories run crushingly into the existing power structure of both Nathan Price and the Congolese governments, and Kingsolver's need to draw the chronology out through the daughters' mature lives enervates any drama that had existed. Once out of Africa, once free from the horrors of punitive political strife, the women of *The Poisonwood Bible* have little adventure left to face. Even Orleanna, who wants only peace and finds it amid her crowded garden on an off-shore Georgia island, has so removed herself from existence that she does not appear admirable. Her sadly plaintive narrative—at the opening of the novel and the opening of each book within it—comes to seem, finally, warped. In Kingsolver's words, she remains "inhumanly alone." Trading what should have been her life for the glimpse of the magical *okapi*, the African unicorn figure, Orleanna claims in her meditations that she did not give her best to her children and her spouse: [S]he was as opportunistic as Nathan. She was in love with Africa:

> Let me claim that Africa and I kept company for a while and then parted ways, as if we were both party to relations with a failed outcome. Or say I was afflicted with Africa like a bout of a rare disease, from which I have not managed a full recovery. Maybe I'll even confess the truth, that I rode in with the horsemen and

beheld the apocalypse, but still I'll insist I was only a captive witness. What is the conqueror's wife, if not a conquest herself? (*Poisonwood*, 9)

The narrative problem of all this information, the five fully drawn and voicing characters set within a political structure familiar to most readers, was holding a reader's attention when there was no sympathetic center. To turn the continent of Africa into a character may have been one of Kingsolver's aims, but the elaborate structure of the book made that difficult. Readers were expecting Orleanna, and probably at least one of the daughters, to carry the weight of the heroic role. That readers appeared to be anything but disappointed in what she had achieved may have been more a tribute to the intricacy of the book than to its final impact.

For Sarah Kerr, writing in *The New York Times Magazine*, *The Poisonwood Bible* was nothing short of a "quantum-leap breakthrough." (Kerr, 52) A *Booklist* reviewer commented on the scope of the novel: "[N]o facet of civilization or the human spirit goes unexplored in this measureless saga of hubris and deliverance." (Seaman, 1922) Compared with the works of Joseph Conrad, Graham Greene, Evelyn Waugh, Nadine Gordimer, Lessing, and Hemingway, as well as with Toni Morrison's *Beloved*, *The Poisonwood Bible* was reviewed in most venues during the autumn of 1998, and the following year it won the National Book Prize of South Africa.[2] It was runner-up for the Pulitzer Prize in Fiction and was a "winning finalist" for the PEN/Faulkner award. It won the Patterson Fiction Prize from the Poetry Center and the American Booksellers Book of the Year Award. It was a finalist for the British Orange Prize, which Kingsolver lost when she did not travel to England for the readings necessary for the award. The novel was a selection of Oprah's Book Club. It was one of the *New York Times* "Ten Best Books of 1998" and the *Los Angeles Times* and *Village Voice* "Best Books for 1998." It appeared on the Canadian North 49 "Valuable Picks" list and on the New York Public Library "25 Books to Remember" list.

The politics of both the author and the novel were becoming more and more visible. The safety Kingsolver had previously found as reviewers discussed her first three novels—*The Bean Trees, Animal Dreams,* and *Pigs in Heaven*—was, with this large compendium of a much-honored book, shattered. No longer was she a domestic novelist who wrote about the Southwest and the South, championing people of color and mixed race in plots secondary to the stories of the women protagonists she crafted. In *The Poisonwood Bible,* Kingsolver appeared fluently political: she knew the issues, she did not like the United States' role in Congolese history, and she did not like the all-encompassing power of the institutional patriarchy of the Church. In this novel, there was no place to hide her opinions.

Those opinions had hardly been kept secret. In her 1984 review of Jonathan Kwitny's book *Endless Enemies* for *The Progressive,* Kingsolver (described in the author's column as a "free-lance writer based in Tucson") complimented him for producing what she called "a definitive source book on ... 'the moral staining of the Constitution': United States intervention of *everywhere* during the last thirty-five years." (Kingsolver, *Progressive* 48, 1983, 44) She agreed with his assessment of American involvement in Zaire: "[W]hat we could do wrong, we did." Even though she objected to Kwitny's sometimes imprecise use of *Marxism, socialism,* and similar terms, she claimed the book was "an eye-opener, even for the initiated reader." (45) Fourteen years later, she published a novel that reinforced Kwitny's assertions.

It is during the mid-1980s (1983–1986, according to David King Dunaway in his interview with Kingsolver) that the FBI conducted "investigations of more than three hundred human rights and community organizations in the United States." (Dunaway, 102) Kingsolver fills in Dunaway's outline:

Among the groups and individuals who were investigated were the Maryknoll nuns, the Quakers (those renowned terrorists), the National Education Association, and me. I got a call at work one day at the University of Arizona. This fellow introduced himself and said, "I'm investigating you for suspicion of international terrorism." ... They tapped our phone. (102)

Her poem of that title was one result; another was her refusal to be intimidated. Kingsolver continued what she described as her "community organizing and educating people about US foreign policy in Latin America." (102) The FBI investigations ended in 1988, the year *The Bean Trees* was published.

Kingsolver's first novel gave reviewers little reason to criticize her for being overly political, or too politically correct. But by the time of *The Poisonwood Bible* a decade later, the author had grown into writing what seemed to be a different kind of fiction. *The Poisonwood Bible* was much longer than any of her earlier books, and it was about formal Christian religion. Africa was not Arizona (or Kentucky or Appalachia); the primary characters were men— Nathan Price and the various leaders of the African villages; and the struggle was far beyond finding rent money or repairing a car so that its owner can get to work. But of course, ultimately too, Kingsolver was writing about the domestic, the relationship among family members, and the need for community. Even the overt political theme was tied, perhaps unnecessarily, into the Price family history: both Patrice Lumumba and Ruth May Price died on January 17, 1961.

There is another coincidence, one that replaces the serious thrust of the novel with irony. One of the rumors that live past Nathan Price's death is that he had five wives, a situation which would have made him a wealthy and respected man, even if a white man; but that all five left him. Taken as part of the Price lore, his daughters thought little of the story until they realized that they, Orleanna and the four of them, were his "five wives." The women who cared for him, who submitted their lives to maintaining his position, were cast in the role of "wife," regardless of their relationship. In the mythic structure of the Congo, none of the women exists—only Nathan. The Price women's situation is as colonial, and as subject to the rules of the patriarchy, as Africa's itself.

When the book was finished and HarperCollins offered her an advance of one million dollars, the sum enabled Kingsolver to bring into being a plan she had long been developing.[3] She was able to establish The Bellwether Prize for Fiction, a large literary award to be given every two years for an excellent manuscript that represented what Kingsolver called the literature of "social justice and the impact of culture and politics on human relationships." (prize advertisement) The $25,000 prize, awarded in 2000 to Donna Gershten for her novel *Kissing the Virgin's Mouth* and in 2002 to Gayle Brandeis for *The Book of Dead Birds*, will be offered again in 2004. Both novels were published by HarperCollins the year after receiving the prize. Judges for the prizes have included Russell Banks, Martin Espada, Ursula K. Le Guin, Maxine Hong Kingston, Toni Morrison, Grace Paley, and Ruth Ozeki.

For Kingsolver, the Bellwether Prize is a legacy she is able to leave the world of readers, ensuring that "socially responsible literature" will be available, regardless of currents in political fashion. The winners of this award will, through their work, depict "a moral obligation of individuals to engage with their communities in ways that promote a more respectful coexistence." (advertisement)

That the prize had itself been funded by Kingsolver's own novel, *The Poisonwood Bible*, was strikingly appropriate. As she had said of her 1998 book, she had wanted it to convey "passion, culpability, anger and a long-term fascination with Africa." (Kingsolver website) And she had wanted it to succeed so well because, in the realm of social justice, she believed "that what happened to the Congo is one of the most important political parables of our century." (website)

CHAPTER TEN

Prodigal Summer, Politics, and Eco-Politics

*Ms. Kingsolver's writing is generously well-crafted;
choice moments ... radiate from nearly every page.*
—*Wall Street Journal*

NOT ALL POLITICAL CONCERNS have to be with nations, wars, and ownership. Even fewer have to do with the conflicts of gender and power, the roles of women juxtaposed with those of men. When Barbara Kingsolver early in her writing career confessed to a number of *-isms*—humanism, feminism, environmentalism—as well as being "a social advocate," she may not have given enough emphasis to one of the most significant: her belief that people could save the planet. (Beattie, ed., 163) She later refers to herself as having developed "a good agrarian state of mind" (*Essential Agrarian Reader*, xvii):

> Sometime around my fortieth birthday, I began an earnest study of agriculture. I worked quietly on this project, speaking of my new interest to almost no one, because of what they might think. Specifically, they might think I was out of my mind.
>
> Why? Because at this moment in history it's considered smart to get out of agriculture.... (ix)

Kingsolver's writing process itself may have played a role in the subject matter of *Prodigal Summer*, her year 2000 novel. After finishing *The Poisonwood Bible*, which had required extensive research on site and in conventional libraries, Kingsolver was interested in writing about something she knew intimately, and cared a great deal about. The child of farmers, she had done her share of chores on a small Kentucky farm, and she still witnessed the struggles of her neighbors to earn a living from their labor. In the larger sense, Kingsolver mentioned often that in the year 1996, more than half the world's population lived in cities rather than on the land or in small towns—and the ratio slanted more heavily toward the urban population with each passing year. In the United States, farming was becoming so rare as to be almost exotic.

She decided to write a novel about the land, and about farming it. She told Noah Adams in a radio interview:

> When researching a setting, you have to know a lot more about a place than you can learn from looking at pictures. You have to know what it smells like after a rain. You have to know the quality of the air, how it feels on your face. You have to know what's blooming in May and how that has changed by July. And you have to know how people are, how they talk. This book [*Prodigal Summer*] is about a county and three months. You can't just visit a place and write about it, in my opinion, not a whole novel. A lie in fiction is a hundred times more boring than a lie in real life. (Adams, 18)

In "a county and three months," Kingsolver gave herself a set of parameters that helped to unify the three separate stories she was going to tell in the novel. With a focus on the lush—i.e., *prodigal*—growing season in the Kentucky–Virginia–West Virginia terrain, she chose stories that were less dependent on a single question than her narratives usually were. Again, to Adams, she said that the novel is about "the biological exigencies of life on Earth[,] ... about the human food chain, the connections between humans and our habitat[,] ... [and] about small farming and the difficulties faced by small farmers." (20)

In *Prodigal Summer,* Kingsolver maps the southern Appalachian terrain by following three characters whose stories, though geographically tangential, seem unconnected. Her aim in this novel is more to make a character from the place, or perhaps from the natural world, than to write conventional narrative. The events in each of the three primary characters' lives stem from the earth, the trees, the animals. They themselves are strangely volitionless human beings.

The strongest narrative of the three is "Predators," the story of Deanna Wolfe, a middle-aged woman who has lived for the two years since her divorce as a ranger in the Zebulon National Forest. No more sensitive and knowing observer of the natural world exists, and she is supremely content with her isolated—and isolating—life. With the opening lines of this section of the book, Kingsolver begins her compelling message that all human and animal life is interrelated: "Her body moved with the frankness that comes from solitary habits. But solitude is only a human presumption. Every quiet step is thunder to beetle life underfoot; every choice is a world made new for the chosen. All secrets are witnessed." (Kingsolver, *Prodigal Summer,* 1)

Kingsolver describes Deanna's search for the animal she is tracking, following her eyes around the "old giant" of a stump, "raggedly rotting its way backward into the ground.... Toadstools dotted the humus at its base, tiny ones, brilliant orange, with delicately ridged caps like open parasols."

The intruder in her life on this occasion is the young hunter (the predator) Eddie Bondo, whose tracking prowess equals hers. Their narrative of impetuous eroticism is complicated by her attempts to keep him from finding and killing the coyote family she has discovered. A hunter, intent on the kill, he is archetypically fixed on accomplishing his aim.

Deanna's secret knowledge of the hidden coyote den—pups, mother, and the several other females—is more important to her than the passion that erupts between her, a woman divorced by "an older husband facing his own age badly and suddenly critical of his wife," and the young Bondo. The delicious young male body—"ferociously beautiful"—gives her pleasure through the summer; "[i]t was the body's decision, a body with no more choice of its natural history than an orchid has...." But the coyote pups grow, and for their safely, she has to make Eddie Bondo leave.

The second book, twined around and between segments of "Predators," is "Moth Love," the story of the brilliant Lusa Maluf Landowski, a young research Ph.D. whose specialization is the study of moths and butterflies. When Cole Widener, an Appalachian farmer, takes one of her seminars and falls in love with her, they marry and she moves to his family farm near Zebulon Mountain. Barely surviving, Cole and his family of five older sisters are faced with an ethical decision: if they give up the tobacco farming which keeps the farm running, what other crop will earn them an adequate income?

Moving from the university in Lexington to the small farming town, Lusa feels her very body divided. She loves Cole, but she also loves her study—"moth love ... *Actias luna, Hyalophora cecropia, Automeris io*, luna, cecropia, Io, the giant saturniid moths." She is lonely.

On the morning of Cole's death in a delivery truck accident, a part-time job he has had to take, they argue over whether or not his brother-in-law killed every animal in a coyote's den. "Every word they said to each other was wrong; every truth underneath it unsayable, unfindable." Lusa's decision to stay on the farm—to not only work it but make it profitable—is her tribute to the wordless love she had shared with Cole.

The third novella, "Old Chestnuts," is the account of the irascible Garnett Walker's fight to keep a few chestnut trees alive. In his rancorous relationship with his unconventional neighbor, Nannie Rawley, he attacks her efforts to save their land; his aim in the first part of the novella is to remove her sign, "No Spray Zone." Nearly eighty, Garnett lives more often in memories of the past—of his grandfather, of his wife who died eight years before, of his students in the country school—except when he is frustrated by Nannie.

Their *rapprochement* comes in the height of summer, the season from which the novel takes its title. Or, in Kingsolver's words, "prodigal summer, the season of extravagant procreation. It could wear out everything in its path with its passionate excesses, but nothing alive with wings or a heart or a seed curled into itself in the ground could resist welcoming it back when it came."

The movement of the separate stories is calendar-based: Kingsolver identifies the time of each alternate segment clearly. The second round of the narratives occurs in later May, the third in June. Each is so rooted in the life of the forest and farm land that description of growth in these different time periods is natural, and accurate. By the end of summer, each plotline has come to a kind of resolution—and has fused with another of the seemingly separate stories.

The elusive totem of the novel is the coyote. Integral to both "Predators" and "Moth Love," the animal finally makes its appearance for Garnett Walker: "There it stood in broad daylight[—] ... a dog, but not a dog. Garnett had never seen the like of it. It was a wild, fawn-colored thing with its golden tail arched high and its hackles standing up and its eyes directly on Garnett." And it is with the female coyote as she prowls the Zebulon Mountain land that *Prodigal Summer* ends. Chapter 31 is a part of none of the three novellas: it is instead a new start, a "sweet, damp night at the beginning of the world."

The world of *Prodigal Summer* is truly the natural world; it is not only the world of Deanna, Lusa, and Garnett. Overshadowed by all the concerns of natural existence, each of them searches for more than a traditionally happy, human life. Kingsolver makes clear their comparative incompleteness. She explains to her readers, "This novel is not exclusively—or even mainly—about humans. There is no main character. My agenda is to lure you into thinking about whole systems, not just individual parts. The story asks for a broader grasp of connections and interdependencies than is usual in our culture." (Kingsolver website)

Using this explanation as a point of departure, the reader can return to one of Deanna's more heated arguments with Eddie, when she tells him she's most interested in coyotes, bobcats, bears, foxes—"Everything that's here. But especially the carnivores." When he asks why she likes best "to watch meat eaters," she rebukes him, "They're the top of the food chain, that's the reason.... If they're good, then their prey is good, and *its* food is good. If not, then something's missing from the chain." She continues, "Keeping tabs on the predators tells you what you need to know about the herbivores, like deer, and the vegetation, the detritivores, the insect populations, small predators like shrews and voles. All of it...." Their discussion also provides a gloss for the title of the first novella, which is "Predators," a plural that links Eddie and Deanna (satisfying each other's sexual needs) with the needs of the coyotes, bear, and foxes, the top-of-the-chain animal predators.

Prodigal Summer is also a book about the losses of life. Garnett has lost his wife, his son, and his grandchildren; Lusa has lost her husband and one of her sisters-in-law; Deanna has lost nearly all connection to other human beings. But as a surrounding pattern of loss for all the characters, Kingsolver creates the realization of the vanishing species throughout the animal kingdom, and Deanna's fight to protect the coyote family is just one visible mark of what seems to be a losing struggle. As the author notes, the story's three main characters are obsessed with what they call ghosts: extinct animals, dispossessed relatives, the American chestnut. In the networks of life described in this story, the absence of a thing is as important as its presence. (website)

Prodigal Summer illustrated for Kingsolver her progress as a novelist: "As writers mature, we tend to deal with increasingly ambitious subjects.... I began with straight-line narratives, and am steadily working up to more complex geometry." About her fifth novel, she explained, "This is the most challenging book I've ever given my readers. Several reviewers have completely missed what the book is about." (website)

With her own great commitment to the natural world, to growing much of her family's food, and to preserving the earth's bounty, Kingsolver saw little difference between pouring her energies into the African novel and into this, her farmland novel. For *Prodigal Summer* is also a political novel, one that calls the reader's attention to the abuses of the land. Reviewers had to change strategies; most found new kinds of things to praise in Kingsolver's work. They liked the characters; they liked the issues; they liked the synergy throughout which brought the seemingly separate story lines into a closely woven tapestry by the end. A runaway bestseller in England as well as the States, *Prodigal Summer* was quickly translated into all the European languages. As a result of this highly successful novel, coming so quickly after the visible and much-praised *The Poisonwood Bible*, Kingsolver was awarded the National Medal for the Humanities by the President of the United States, William J. Clinton.

As Kingsolver herself had predicted, there were a few reviewers who saw this more scientific book as less political. They were not sure the Appalachian setting was as significant as the African. For the author, however, *Prodigal Summer* "was a matter of coming home to my own language and culture." (Kingsolver website) *Prodigal Summer* was more aligned with *Animal Dreams*, her second book which had been praised for its efforts to create ecological understanding, and had won the Edward Abbey Ecofiction Award. As Paula Gunn Allen discusses the Southwest and its literature, one determining factor is a "bedrock of a particular kind of Native American civilization[,] ... a particular aesthetic that is rooted in an ongoing relationship, a conversation, among the human, the plant and animal, the land, and the supernaturals, each perceived as members of the same geospiritual community." (Allen, xxi) In *Prodigal Summer*, Kingsolver succeeded in moving this geospiritual community east.

Compared with other of Kingsolver's works, *Prodigal Summer* also does more to make sexuality a natural part of its characters' lives. Procreation occupies the heart of the natural world, but, as Kingsolver notes, "Sex in our strange culture is both an utter taboo and the currency of jaded commerce." (website) She said to Noah Adams, "Some people might be taken aback by how sexy this book is[,] ... but I had to risk it. There are difficult things about it because the language of coition has pretty much been divvied up between pornography and the medical profession.... So the challenge is to invent a new poetry of copulation and then to write it without blushing." (Adams, 21) In a recent essay, she continues, "Great sex is rarer in art than life because it's harder to do. To broach the subject of sex at all, writers must first face down the polite pretense that it doesn't really matter to us, and acknowledge that in the grand scheme of things, few things could matter more." (*Small Wonder*, 227)

Prodigal Summer follows in the Kingsolver tradition of attempting to answer yet another set of important questions. Those questions differ book by book, and in each novel, she tries to bring her readers new information, new insights about the human and the animal, the political, and the spiritual condition. As she wrote in another recent essay, "Literature should inform as well as enlighten, and first, do no harm.... The business of fiction is to probe the tender spots of an imperfect world, which is where I live, write, and read." (*Small Wonder*, 213)

Small Wonder and *Last Stand*:
America's Virgin Lands

KINGSOLVER'S IMPERFECT WORLD REACHED its nadir on September 11, 2001, with the terrorist attack on the United States. Stunned by the brutality and the resulting loss of lives and the decimation of cities, as were most Americans, Kingsolver turned to her writing in response. On September 12, she was asked to become one voice of her dismayed country, to prepare an opinion piece for a metropolitan newspaper. Accordingly, on that day, she took it upon herself to write an essay about not only the horrific tragedy but also about the enduring promise of the United States.

Small Wonder, with its characteristically modest title and the by now familiar line drawings by the artist and illustrator Paul Mirocha, was published by HarperCollins in the autumn of the following year. All Kingsolver's royalties from this collection of essays are allocated to four charities: Environmental Defense, Habitat for Humanity, Physicians for Social Responsibility, and Heifer International.

Kingsolver wrote in the foreword to *Small Wonder*, "I learned a surprising thing in writing this book. It is possible to move away from a vast, unbearable pain by delving into it deeper and deeper." (Kingsolver website) With reference to Adrienne Rich's seminal poem, "Diving into the Wreck," Kingsolver shared with her readers her lament for her country, the initial sense of personal betrayal and fear, and the cumulative effects of what she called "the strange, awful time that dawned on us." By her account, first she wrote the first essay that had been requested. Then she wrote another, and another: "Sometimes writing seemed to be all that kept me from falling apart in the face of so much death and anguish, the one alternative to weeping without cease."

Several of these new essays were about the American flag, pristine in its symbolic and encouraging role for the broken culture. Unfortunately, and perhaps unintentionally, another columnist quoted one of Kingsolver's sentences from that somewhat ironically patriotic piece and left out several words. The quoted sentence "said" the opposite of what Kingsolver's sentence had said. In a very short time, commentators who were looking to the world of words in the hope of sorting through the political left and the political right, rather than for any general outcry of sorrow, had charged Barbara Kingsolver with making unpatriotic statements.

Several journalists came to her defense. When David Gates wrote "The Voices of Dissent" for *Newsweek* in November, he grouped Kingsolver with Susan Sontag and Arundhati Roy; the former had been attacked for her criticism of President Bush, the latter for her novel *The God of Small Things*. (Gates, 66–67) Gates pointed out that Kingsolver's dissent, if it could even be called that, is "both moral and practical" when she calls for the effort to "recapture [the] flag from the men now waving it in the name of jingoism and censorship." He quoted Kingsolver's repeated words: " 'I speak out because I love my country and want to do the right thing.' " A few months later, Steve Flairty's "Barbara Kingsolver— Kentucky's 'Polite Firebrand' Author" placed her in the company of Wendell Berry and the late Harriette Arnow. (Flairty, 12–15)

By that time, the controversy was over. As Kingsolver recalled, mail deluged her Arizona office: readers wrote to ask her if she had, indeed, been critical; others wrote to say they remained loyal (and book sales for *Prodigal Summer* were higher than for any of her earlier books). A few, however, wrote "very violent, very fanatical, very self-righteous" (Rehm interview)—very threatening—missives to her, and she and her family feared for what might result from this wholesale anger. "You stand up for what you believe is right," she told Diane Rehm on a 2002 radio show; in the climate of the terrorist attack, however, "political" had become an even more highly charged word.

With two exceptions ("Letter to My Mother" and "Letter to a Daughter at Thirteen"), the essays in *Small Wonder* are less personal than those of *High Tide in Tucson*. "Flying," "Knowing Our Place," "Life Is Precious, or It's Not," "And Our Flag Was Still There," and others all discuss in some way the September 11 tragedy, or circumstances that may have led to it. In the collection's closing essay, "God's Wife's Measuring Spoons," Kingsolver describes the fact of her being "misquoted in inflammatory ways" and thanks her readers for standing by her. (*Small Wonder*, 249) Several of the essays about the natural world were collaborative efforts with her ornithologist spouse; several others were congruent with the crisply poetic prose commentary she had written to accompany the remarkable photographs of Annie Griffiths Belt, published in 2002 as the large-format photo book *Last Stand: America's Virgin Lands*, by the National Geographic Press. In this study of the five kinds of virgin lands remaining—wetlands, woodlands, coasts, grasslands, and drylands—Kingsolver pays tribute to William Bartram, John Muir, Henry David Thoreau, Aldo Leopold, Edward Abbey, and Rachel Carson, among other writers who were also conservationists. Her foreword to *The Essential Agrarian Reader*, written in the following year, continues many of the themes she probes in *Last Stand*.

The fact that Kingsolver's work is so clearly all of a piece gives her encomium from one of the *Small Wonder* essays a lingering resonance: "My way of finding a place in this world is to write one. This work is less about making a living, really, than about finding a way to be alive...." (*Small Wonder*, 233)

■ NOTES

FOREWORD NOTES

* These and other quotations are from an unpublished, 100-page, 1992 interview I conducted for a book and radio documentary series, *Writing the Southwest.*[1]

1. David Dunaway, "Barbara Kingsolver," *Writing the Southwest* (New York: Plume, 1995; Albuquerque: University of New Mexico Press, 2003.

2. John Bergeron, interview, "In These Times," May 21, 1980.

3. David Dunaway, *Aldous Huxley Recollected* (Walnut Creek: Altamira Press, 1998).

4. Doris Lessing, *The Four-Gated City* (New York: Alfred Knopf, 1969), pp. 493–495.

CHAPTER NOTES

1. Kingsolver web bibliography, Technical and Scientific Writing; see also other publications, as second author, "Chapter Nine: Production of Resins by Arid-Adapted Astereae" in *Phytochemical Adaptations to Stress* (Plenum Publishing, 1984) and as sole author of Chapter 18 in *Arid Lands: Communities and Legacies* (1985 and 1986).

2. See John Leonard, "Kingsolver in the Jungle, Catullus and Wolfe at the Door," *Nation* 268, no. 2, January 11–18, 1999, p. 28; Gayle Greene, "Independence Struggle," *Women's Review of Books* 16, no. 7, April, 1999; and Verlyn Klinkenborg, "Going Native," *New York Times Book Review,* October 18, 1998, p. 7.

3. *Publishers Weekly* (February l0, 1997) carried an item that implied Kingsolver was thinking of leaving HarperCollins because the firm published books by conservative politicians. When the author replied (April 7, 1997), she praised her publishers for "NEVER" trying to change her work.

Adams, Noah. Interview with Barbara Kingsolver, "All Things Considered," October 23, 2000. Washington, D. C.: National Public Radio, 2000.

Allen, Paula Gunn. "Preface to *Writing the Southwest*," ed. David King Dunaway and Sara L. Spurgeon. Albuquerque: University of New Mexico Press, 2004, pp. xvii–xxiv.

Aulette, Judy and Trudy Mills. "Something Old, Something New: Auxiliary Work in the 1983–1986 Copper Strike," *Feminist Studies*, Summer, 1988, pp. 251–68.

Barbara Kingsolver, Signatures film, Annenberg/CPB.

Barbara Kingsolver website.

Beattie, L. Elisabeth, ed. "Barbara Kingsolver interview" in *Conversations with Kentucky Writers*. Lexington: University of Kentucky Press, 1996, pp. 150–71.

Bowdan, Janet. "Re-placing Ceremony: The Poetics of Barbara Kingsolver," *Southwestern American Literature* 20, no. 2, Spring, 1995, pp. 13–19.

Butler, Jack. "She Hung the Moon and Plugged in All the Stars," *New York Times Book Review*, April 10, 1988, p. 15.

Charles, Ron. "Review of Prodigal Summer," *Christian Science Monitor* 92, no. 230 (October 19, 2000), p. 20.

Dunaway, David King and Sara L. Spurgeon, ed. *Writing the Southwest*. Albuquerque: University of New Mexico Press, 2004, pp. 93–108.

Epstein, Robin. "The Progressive Interview: Barbara Kingsolver," *The Progressive*, February, 1996, pp. 33–37.

Fitzgerald, Karen. "Review of *The Bean Trees*," *Ms.*, April 1988, p. 28.

Flairty, Steve. "Barbara Kingsolver—Kentucky's 'Polite Firebrand' Author," *Kentucky Monthly*, February, 2002, pp. 12–15.

Gates, David. "The Voices of Dissent," *Newsweek*, November 19, 2001, pp. 66–67.

Giles, Jeff. "Review of *Prodigal Summer*," *Newsweek* 136, October 30, 2000, p. 82.

Holt, Patricia. "Review of *The Bean Trees*," *San Francisco Chronicle*, March 6, 1988, p. 1.

Jones D. and J.D. Jorgenson. *Contemporary Authors: New Revised Series*. Detroit: Gale, 1998.

Kerr, Sarah. "The Novel as Indictment," *New York Times Magazine*, October 11, 1998, pp. 52–56.

Kingsolver, Barbara and Annie Griffiths Belt. *Last Stand: America's Virgin Lands*. Washington, D. C.: National Geographic Society, 2002.

Kingsolver, Barbara and Jill Barrett Fein," Women on the Line," *The Progressive*, March, 1984, p. 15.

Marsh, Dave, ed. *Mid-Life Confidential*. New York: Viking, 1994.

Pence, Amy. "An Interview with Barbara Kingsolver," *Poets & Writers*, July/August, 1993, pp. 14–21.

Perry, Donna, ed. "Interview with Barbara Kingsolver," *Back Talk: Women Writers Speak Out*. New Brunswick: Rutgers University Press, 1993, pp. 143–69.

Quinn, Judy. "Book News: Harper-Collins Gets to Keep Kingsolver," *Publishers Weekly*, February 10, 1997, p. 19.

Randall, Margaret. "Human Comedy," *Women's Review of Books* 5, no. 8, May, 1988, pp. 1, 3.

Rehm, Diane. "Interview with Barbara Kingsolver, November 5, 1998." Washington, D. C.: WAMU, American University.

———. "Interview with Barbara Kingsolver, May 14, 2002." Washington, D. C.: WAMU, American University.

Rosenblum, Jonathan D. *Copper Crucible: How the Arizona Miners' Strike of 1983 Recast Labor-Management Relations in America*. Ithaca, New York: ILR/Cornell University Press, 1995 and 1998.

Seaman, Donna. "The Poisonwood Bible," *Booklist*, August 10, 1998, p.1922.

Smiley, Jane. "In One Small Town, the Weight of the World," *New York Times Book Review*, September 2, 1990, p. 2.

1955   Barbara Ellen Kingsolver, second child of Virginia Henry and Wendell Kingsolver, is born.

1960   Her sister Ann is born.

1963   Dr. Kingsolver takes his family on a medical mission to the Congo.

1968   Dr. Kingsolver takes his family on a medical mission to St. Lucia; Barbara begins serious study of the piano with teachers in Lexington.

1972   Kingsolver studies music at the University of Kentucky, summer school.

1973   She graduates valedictorian from Nicholas County High School and begins college at DePauw University (Greencastle, Indiana) on a scholarship in piano performance.

1975   She spends her junior year abroad in Greece and France.

1977   Kingsolver graduates *magna cum laude* from DePauw and returns to Europe.

1978   She moves to Tucson, Arizona, and works as a medical technologist.

1981   Kingsolver takes a master's degree from the University of Arizona, rather than continue in the doctoral program in biology and ecology there.

1982–85   Scientific publications; works on campus as a science writer; covers Phelps Dodge copper miners' strike.

1985   Marries Joseph Hoffman, a professor at the University of Arizona.

1986   Wins Arizona Press Club Award for journalism.

1987   Daughter Camille is born.

1988   *The Bean Trees* is published by HarperCollins.

1989   *Homeland and Other Stories* is published by HarperCollins; *Holding the Line: Women in the Great Arizona Mine Strike*, by ILR, Cornell University Press.

1990   *Animal Dreams* is published by HarperCollins.

1991   Lives in the Canary Islands.

1992   *Another America/Otra America*, poems, is published by
       Seal Press; visits Japan; plays with authors' band, the Rock
       Bottom Remainders.

1993   *Pigs in Heaven* is published by HarperCollins.

1994   Marries Steven Hopp, ornithologist and musician.

1995   *High Tide in Tucson* (essays) is published by
       HarperCollins; receives honorary doctorate from DePauw
       University.

1996   Second daughter, Lily, is born.

1998   *The Poisonwood Bible* is published by HarperCollins; the
       Bellwether Prize is established.

2000   *Prodigal Summer* is published by HarperCollins; receives
       National Humanities Medal from President Clinton.

2001   Writes a number of essays after the destruction of 9/11.

2002   *Small Wonder* (essays) is published by HarperCollins; *Last
       Stand: America's Virgin Lands* is published by National
       Geographic, with the photos of Annie Griffiths Belt.

"World of Foes," *The Progressive* (1983)

The Bean Trees (1988)

Homeland and Other Stories (1989)

Holding the Line: Women in the Great Arizona Mine Strike of 1983 (1989; 1996, 2nd edition, introduction by Kingsolver)

Animal Dreams (1990)

Another America/Otra America. Spanish translations by Rebeca Cartes. (1992; 1998, 2nd edition, Foreword by Margaret Randall; Introduction by Kingsolver).

"Secret Animals," *Turnstile* 3 (1992).

"Introduction," *Southwest Stories: Tales from the Desert,* ed. John Miller and Genevieve Morgan (1993)

Pigs in Heaven (1993)

"Confessions of the Reluctant Remainder," *Mid-Life Confidential,* ed. Dave Marsh (1994)

High Tide in Tucson, Essays from Now or Never (1995)

"Barbara Kingsolver, Dear Mom," *I've Always Meant to Tell You: Letters to Our Mothers/An Anthology of Contemporary Women Writers,* ed. Constance Warloe (1997)

"Kingsolver Clarifies," *Publishers Weekly* (1997)

The Poisonwood Bible (1998)

"Journeys," *Paris Review* 153 (Winter 2000)

Prodigal Summer (2000)

Small Wonder (2002)

Foreword, *Essential Agrarian Reader* (2003)

Adams, Noah. Interview with Barbara Kingsolver, "All Things Considered," October 23, 2000. Washington, D.C.: National Public Radio, 2000.

Allen, Paula Gunn. "Preface to *Writing the Southwest*," ed. David King Dunaway and Sara L. Spurgeon. New York: Penguin, 1995, pp. xvii–xxiv.

Aulette, Judy and Trudy Mills. "Something Old, Something New: Auxiliary Work in the 1983–1986 Copper Strike," *Feminist Studies*, Summer, 1988, pp. 251–68.

Barbara Kingsolver, Signatures film, Annenberg/CPB

Basso, K. " 'Speaking with names': Language and Landscape among the Western Apache," *Rereading Cultural Anthropology*, ed. G. Marcus. Durham: Duke University Press, 1992, pp. 220–51.

Beattie, L. Elisabeth, ed. "Barbara Kingsolver interview" in *Conversations with Kentucky Writers*. Lexington: University of Kentucky Press, 1996, pp. 150–71.

Bowdan, Janet. "Re-placing Ceremony: The Poetics of Barbara Kingsolver," *Southwestern American Literature* 20, no. 2, Spring, 1995, pp. 13–19.

Brandeis, Gayle. *The Book of Dead Birds* (Bellwether Prize). New York: HarperCollins, 2003.

Butler, Jack. "She Hung the Moon and Plugged in All the Stars," *New York Times Book Review*, April 10, 1988, p. 15.

Charles, Ron. "Review of *Prodigal Summer*," *Christian Science Monitor* 92, no. 230 (October 19, 2000), p. 20.

Dunaway, David King and Sara L. Spurgeon, ed. *Writing the Southwest*. New York: Penguin, 1995, pp. 93–108.

Epstein, Robin. " *The Progressive* Interview: Barbara Kingsolver," *The Progressive*, February, 1996, pp. 33–37.

Fitzgerald, Karen. "Review of *The Bean Trees*," *Ms.*, April 1988, p. 28.

Flairty, Steve. "Barbara Kingsolver—Kentucky's 'Polite Firebrand' Author," *Kentucky Monthly*, February, 2002, pp. 12–15.

Gates, David. "The Voices of Dissent," *Newsweek*, November 19, 2001, pp. 66–67.

Gershten, Donna M. *Kissing the Virgin's Mouth* (Bellwether Prize). New York: HarperCollins, 2001.

Giles, Jeff. "Review of *Prodigal Summer*," Newsweek 136, October 30, 2000, p. 82.

Greene, Gayle. "Independence Struggle," *Women's Review of Books* 16, no. 7, April, 1999.

Holt, Patricia. "Review of *The Bean Trees*," *San Francisco Chronicle*, March 6, 1988, p. 1.

Kerr, Sarah. "The Novel as Indictment," *New York Times Magazine*, October 11, 1998, pp. 52–56.

Klinkenborg, Verlyn. "Going Native," *New York Times Book Review*, October 18, 1998, p. 7.

Leonard, John. "Kingsolver in the Jungle, Catullus and Wolfe at the Door," *Nation* 268, January 11–18, 1999, p. 28.

Marsh, Dave, ed. *Mid-Life Confidential.* New York: Viking, 1994.

Pence, Amy. "An Interview with Barbara Kingsolver," *Poets & Writers*, July/August, 1993, pp. 14–21.

Perry, Donna, ed. "Interview with Barbara Kingsolver," *Back Talk: Women Writers Speak Out.* New Brunswick: Rutgers University Press, 1993, pp. 143–69.

Quinn, Judy. "Book News: Harper-Collins Gets to Keep Kingsolver," *Publishers Weekly*, February 10, 1997, p. 19.

Randall, Margaret. "Human Comedy," *Women's Review of Books* 5, no. 8, May, 1988, pp. 1, 3.

Rehm, Diane. "Interview with Barbara Kingsolver, November 5, 1998." Washington, D.C.: WAMU, American University.

———. "Interview with Barbara Kingsolver, May 14, 2002." Washington, D.C.: WAMU, American University.

Rosenblum, Jonathan D. *Copper Crucible: How the Arizona Miners' Strike of 1983 Recast Labor-Management Relations in America.* Ithaca, New York: ILR/Cornell University Press, 1995 and 1998.

Schuessler, Jennifer. "Men, Women and Coyotes," *New York Times Book Review*, November 5, 2000, p. 38.

Seaman, Donna. "*The Poisonwood Bible*," *Booklist*, August 10, 1998, p. 1922.

Siegel, Lee. "Review of *The Poisonwood Bible*," *New Republic* 220, no. 12, March 22, 1999, p. 30.

Skow, John. "Review of *The Poisonwood Bible*," *Time* 152, November 9, 1998, p. 19.

Smiley, Jane. "In One Small Town, the Weight of the World," *New York Times Book Review*, September 2, 1990, p. 2.

Wagner-Martin, Linda. Barbara Kingsolver's *The Poisonwood Bible*. New York: Continuum, 2000.

WEBSITES

HarperCollin's Kingsolver website.
www.kingsolver.com

New York Times Featured Author: Barbara Kingsolver
http://www.nytimes.com/books/98/10/18/specials/kingsolver.html

Barnes & Noble Meet the Writers: Barbara Kingsolver
http://www.barnesandnoble.com/writers/writer.asp?cid=883418

Lit Chat with Barbara Kingsolver
http://www.salon.com/16dec1995/departments/litchat.html

KYLIT–A Site devoted to Kentucky Writers
http://www.english.eku.edu/SERVICES/KYLIT/KINGSLVR.HTM

CONTRIBUTORS

Most noted for her groundbreaking biography on Sylvia Plath, LINDA WAGNER-MARTIN is the Frank Borden Hanes Professor of English and Comparative Literature at the University of North Carolina, Chapel Hill. She is the editor and author of over 50 books, including her recent titles *The Portable Edith Wharton* and *William Faulkner: Six Decades of Criticism.* She is also the author of biographies on Gertrude Stein and Ellen Glasgow.

DAVID KING DUNAWAY is the author of a half-dozen volumes of biography and history; he is Professor of English at the University of New Mexico and a frequent lecturer on the literature of the American Southwest.